Aza's Story

An inspiring tale of love and war

Sue McCauley

**Original Interviews:
Judith Paviell**

BANTAM BOOKS
SYDNEY • AUCKLAND • TORONTO • NEW YORK • LONDON

Dedication

To Alida, and to all those children
who suffered in Bosnia during the war.

AZA'S STORY
A BANTAM BOOK

Published in Australia in 1997 by Bantam
First published in New Zealand in 1996 by
Shoal Bay Press Ltd Box 2151, Christchurch,
New Zealand

Copyright © by Aza and Brent King 1996, 1997
and Shoal Bay Press Ltd, 1996, 1997

All rights reserved. No Part of this publication may be reproduced, stored in a retrieval system, transmitted in any form or by any means, electronic, mechanical, photocopying, recording or otherwise, without the prior written permission of the publisher.

National Library of Australia.
Cataloguing-in-Publication Entry

King, Aza.
Aza's story

ISBN 0 7338 0078 5

1. King, Aza. 2. Muslims - Bosnia and Herzegovina - Biography.
3. Yugoslav War 1991 -- Bosnia and Herzegovina.
I McCauley, Sue. II Paviell, Judith. III Title

297.092

Bantam Books are published by

Transworld Publishers (Aust) Pty Limited
15-25 Helles Ave, Moorebank, NSW 2170

Cover design by Azzopardi & Partners
Cover photograph by Helena Hughes
Typeset by DOCUPRO
Printed by McPherson's Printing Group, Victoria

10 9 8 7 6 5 4 3 2 1

Contents

Historical Background	vi
Prologue	xiii
Part 1: Aza	1
1. Spring, 1992	3
2. Summer, 1992	23
3. Winter, 1992-93	46
4. Summer, 1993	71
Part 2: Brent	79
5. Bosnia	80
6. Zepa	97
Part 3: Aza and Brent	119
7. Meeting	120
8. The Plan	147
9. The Escape	176
10. Freedom	213
Epilogue	242

Acknowledgements

We would like to thank our family and friends in New Zealand who first suggested a book describing our Bosnian experiences, then continued to motivate us with their warm support and advice.

The book itself could never have been written without the help of many people. Judith Paviell's gentle, perceptive questions encouraged us to talk freely, filling tape after tape, which Julie Smith swiftly transcribed onto over 600 single-spaced pages, from which Sue McCauley then wrote the book you have today. Sue's was an extraordinarily difficult task, performed under great pressure, and we are very lucky that so fine a writer was able to help us in this way.

We would also like to thank Anna Rogers for editing the text; Naylor Hillary for providing the brief history of Bosnia; and David Elworthy, Luke Elworthy and Ros Henry of Shoal Bay Press for their help, encouragement and enormous enthusiasm for the book.

Words cannot express our gratitude towards Indira, Sanela, Sergey and Robert, without whose active assistance, often at great risk to themselves, Aza would never have reached safety.

Some names in this story have been changed to protect the identities of the people concerned.

We wish to state that the views expressed in this book are our personal views only, and not those of the United Nations, the New Zealand defence forces or any other official body.

Brent and Aza King

Historical Background

No territory has a more troubled history than Bosnia. This is a land about a third the size of New Zealand's South Island, broken and mountainous, with few natural frontiers and with no effective outlet to the sea.

In medieval times it was ruled intermittently by Croats and Serbs, Hungarians and Byzantines. When the Turks conquered Byzantium in 1453 Bosnia was an independent kingdom within the Eastern Roman Empire. In 1463 Bosnia's last independent king was beheaded by the Turks, who then effectively ruled the country until 1878.

In the fifteenth century a mosaic of peoples and religions lived in Bosnia. Slavs were the dominant race, Roman Catholicism and Orthodox Christianity the principal religions. Many Bosnians, however, followed the Bulgarian Bogomil heresy of Christianity and had been persecuted for their faith. The Turks put a stop to the persecution, and as a result many Bogomils grew close to their Turkish rulers and converted to Islam. From then on Muslims supplied the land-owning and administrative élite for the next 400 years. Thus Bosnia developed a class that was Slav by race but Muslim by religion, ruling over a people still largely Slav, but Christian by religion.

This curious ruling class was suppressed, but not destroyed, first by a Turkish army in 1850, and then by Austrian rule. Austria formally annexed Bosnia in 1908, and imposed a new parliament that tried to balance the competing religious and ethnic populations of Bosnia. But many Bosnian Serbs, unhappy about continuing Muslim and Croat influence, looked to the small independent state of Serbia for assistance.

One result was the Black Hand, a revolutionary Serb secret society that spawned Gavrilo Princip, a young Bosnian revolutionary who assassinated Austria's Archduke Ferdinand in Sarajevo on 28 June 1914, thus firing the fuse that a month later sparked the beginning of the First World War.

In 1918 a 'Yugo-slavia', a state for all the southern Slavs formerly ruled by the old Austro-Hungarian Empire, was formed. Bosnia, the geographic heart of the new state, was swept along, with little consultation. But the new unified Yugoslavia soon ran into ethnic trouble, with deputies shooting and killing one another during parliamentary sessions in the capital, Belgrade. King Alexander, a Serb, took over supreme power in 1929 until his assassination in 1934, when the country was run by a regency until his young son Peter became old enough to assume power.

Although Yugoslavia was groping towards a new federal constitution when the country was overwhelmed by the Second World War, it is doubtful whether such a formal arrangement could have worked. Already by the late 1930s the Croat minority in Bosnia had expressed a wish to join Croatia, the larger Serb element wanted union with Serbia, and the Muslims desired Bosnian autonomy, and if this were not possible union with Croatia rather than Serbia.

After the Germans invaded Yugoslavia in 1941 two resistance movements emerged. The Cetniks enjoyed the backing of King Peter's government-in-exile in Britain, while the communist partisans, led by a Croat metalworker known as Tito, fought at first under the instructions of Moscow. By 1944, however, the Allies were supporting Tito, who proclaimed a federal provisional government.

The subsequent history of Bosnia, and Yugoslavia, under communism was a record of gradual liberalisation from the rigid Stalinism of the 1940s. Bosnia benefited from Tito's economic policies, but remained a mix in which the Muslims were an anomaly, under-represented in the administration and conscious that they were still regarded as undesirables by much of Serb Yugoslavia. Tito did, however, foster Muslim power in Bosnia and Herzegovina in an effort to counter the growing ethnic tension between Serbs and Croats. Thus Slav Muslims were granted a distinct ethnic status in the census and were able to participate in the rotating collective state presidency when it was established in 1971.

Under Tito's powerful personality the Yugoslav federation remained intact; it was only after his death in 1980 that disillusionment with political stagnation and economic decline set in throughout the country. By 1990 Bosnia's neighbouring nationalisms of Serbia and Croatia had become intimidating presences, especially as both could claim a degree of loyalty from many Bosnians. Croat and Serb political parties emerged in Bosnia in the same year, and it was only the Muslims who emphasised that they stood for the preservation of

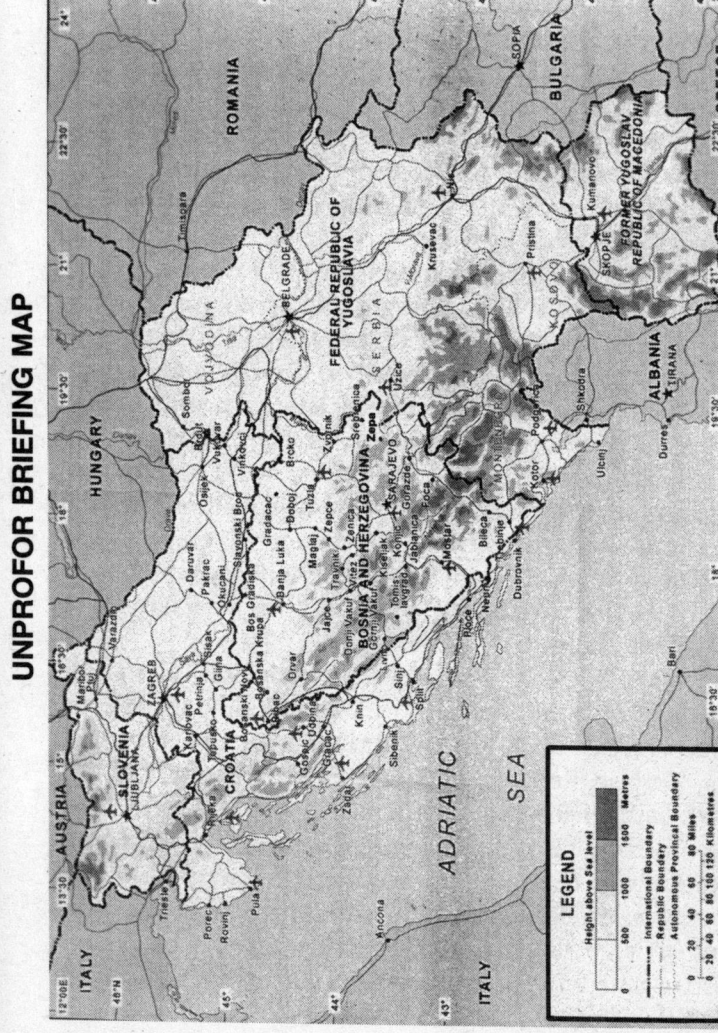

Bosnia's unique character as a multi-national, multi-religious republic. Far from being fundamentalist in outlook, the Muslims were, and are, among the most westernised followers of Islam.

Slovenia and Croatia declared themselves fully independent from the Yugoslav federation on 25 June 1991. Both resisted attacks by the Serb-dominated federal army. Croatia soon lost control of Serb-controlled areas of its territory, while from Belgrade came pronouncements that the Bosnian Croats were only Roman Catholic Serbs, the Muslims only Muslim Serbs, and that both groups should be brought into an enlarged Serbia.

The Bosnian government, headed by a Muslim, tried to maintain a neutrality between Croatia and Serbia – like having to choose between leukemia and a brain tumour, said Bosnia's President Alija Izetbegovic.

Early in 1992 a referendum was held in Bosnia to determine its future, the outcome of which – in spite of Serb attempts to enforce a boycott on voting – was a majority vote for 'a sovereign and independent Bosnia-Herzegovina, a state of equal citizens and nations of Muslims, Serbs, Croats and others'.

On 6 April 1992 Bosnia was recognised as an independent state by the European community, its first full independence since 1463. But at the same time a competing 'Serbian Republic of Bosnia-Herzegovina' comprising Serb-held territories of the republic was also established. Serbia, claiming to be the rump of the old Yugoslav federal government, continued to encourage Serb separatist movements inside Bosnia, with the result that open war broke out between the factions. On 7 July 1992 a breakaway Croat state, covering thirty per cent of the territory of Bosnia-Herzegovina, was also established.

The plight of the Bosnian government was not helped first by an international arms embargo that prevented Bosnia, but not Serbia, from buying arms, and secondly by interference from the European community and the United Nations, which tried to give ethnic labels to districts of Bosnia, heightening the competition for territory and finally setting Croats and Muslims against one another when their unity was the only possible buffer to Serb aggression.

By late 1992, the UN forces were attempting to protect aid convoys and to protect refugees through a series of 'safe areas', one of the smallest of which was Zepa, close to the border with Serbia. It will be clear as Aza and Brent's remarkable story unfolds that effective protection for the Bosnian enclaves became virtually impossible. Refugees poured into the safe areas where both they and the local inhabitants lived in appalling conditions, relying on occasional food convoys and irregular air drops to survive.

Attempts to impose exclusion zones for Serb heavy weapons, especially around Sarajevo, were frustrated by rules that stopped effective air strikes by NATO aircraft. Finally, in May 1995, NATO forces were given permission to retaliate against the Serbs around Sarajevo. In response, the Serb forces took hostages from the UN forces; when the air strikes stopped, the hostages were released.

This pattern was repeated in July as the Serbs advanced against the town of Srebrenica, the largest of the Muslim enclaves. This time they took Dutch servicemen hostage to stop air strikes. The town fell and several thousand inhabitants were massacred. Zepa fell soon afterwards, with similar loss of life.

In August 1995, after a particularly savage Serb mortar attack, the air strikes were resumed round Sarajevo in an effort to compel the Serbs to withdraw the heavy weapons that had been shelling the city for months. After two weeks the Serbs complied.

This backdown, coupled with more aggressive fighting from Bosnia's Croat and Muslim forces confronting the Serbs, encouraged the factions to an international conference in Geneva in September 1995. There the principle of the division of Bosnia into areas or cantons controlled by the three competing ethnic groups was recognised.

The Geneva conference displayed a commitment to maintaining Bosnia-Herzegovina as a sovereign state, but recognised the de facto division into three competing factions, each with its own territory. There followed three months of shuttle diplomacy leading to an agreement at Dayton, Ohio, in November 1995.

The Dayton Accord, as it became known, divided the territory of Bosnia into proportions of fifty-one per cent for the Muslims and Croats, and forty-nine per cent for the Serbs. It promised a new constitution, elections, protection of human rights, return of refugees to their homes, compensation for property loss, and freedom of movement between the three ethnic zones. President Clinton promised US troops for a year and a NATO force of 60,000 was introduced to police the settlement.

After the fighting in Bosnia had died down, late in 1995, the devastated country had a population of about 2.9 million, reduced from 4.4 million five years before. Of the population in 1995, about 1.3 million were Muslims, about 900,000 were Serbs and about 510,000 were Croats.

On all sides there was war weariness and an acceptance of a partitioning of Bosnia that began to look permanent. But even with the huge NATO presence, ethnic cleansing continued, with up to 90,000 people being forced out of their homes in the nine months to September 1996.

Prologue

Our war was a pack of dogs snarling and biting over one bone. One of those dogs was big, sleek and strong; the other was small and unfit from having been too long on a chain. That second dog was us.

'No matter how much they like you,' my grandfather said, 'or how nicely they treat you, or how well you think that you know them, you will never really know what is going on deep, deep down in their hearts. There is a part of them they keep sealed away. You can never totally trust a Serb.'

That, he'd told me, was a lesson he'd learnt in the Second World War. For a long time I thought it was just an old man's prejudice, but now I saw it was true. Serbs would lie to you through smiling jaws, making promises they never intended to keep. They would raise your hopes just for the pleasure of smashing them down again.

That's how it felt to all of us who were trapped in Zepa. They had us captured and on our knees, begging for food, begging for freedom, begging to stay alive.

'Say please!' they were telling us.

'Please,' we would chorus.

Then they would laugh in our faces.

When, at last, we learned that the aid convoys were coming with food, the Serb soldiers waited until we could hear those trucks – and then turned them back. They sent them to a Serb town and claimed the food for their own people. Time after time they turned those convoys back and, when they did let them through the trucks would arrive half empty because the Serbs had helped themselves. Their people, they said, were hungry. Maybe they were, but in Zepa we were starving to death.

In war you see people as they really are, and the truth may be the opposite to what you would expect. When that food did get through, it wasn't fairly distributed; our own townspeople would get there first, and those of us who lived further out in the villages would miss out. 'Those who stand closest to the fire,' my grandfather used to say, 'get all the heat.'

When fear and hunger set in, people forgot the ties of friendship and looked out for their own families, but as fear grew, and the likelihood of dying increased, even family members could be forgotten; people then thought only of keeping themselves alive.

In my own life I had been more fortunate than many. I didn't imagine it made me better than my friends, and I'd tried always to share what I had with others. But there were some people who, until the war began, had thought themselves big shots. Because they owned a large house with new carpets and nice furniture, they would look down on and sneer at their neighbours' little houses and worn mats and shabby possessions. But when that big house had been destroyed and those big shots needed a roof over their heads, the neighbours' shabby little house would suddenly look very beautiful and desirable. Now they would plead to come in and share that house.

I liked to see that happening; it was the only thing about war that gave me satisfaction.

War is like winter, I would tell myself, it has to pass. And after winter there is spring. There is new grass beneath my feet, and wild buttercups and white daisies. There is the smell of fresh growth and life. In spring my emotions will uncurl.

One spring came and went, but the war was not over. The second spring came, and I was in love, but we were not together. My emotions were like a balloon over which I had no control; one moment they would go up, up, up, until they were out of sight, the next moment *whooooof* – deflated, and I would be crying.

I had so many things to cry about, so many questions and accusations. The first was the war. Why had it happened? Why should war ever happen?

Then there was Brent. Why did I have to meet him? Why couldn't I be with him? Why did we keep in touch with each other when it was so hopeless? Wouldn't it be better to have no contact with him and just try to get over it?

Some day, I would tell myself when my mood plunged to zero, you might meet somebody here who you could be happy with. Perhaps it is just the fact that he is from the outside world that attracts you to him? Isn't it true that he's the only person you really know who is free to live a normal life?

Then I would hate myself. How could I think such things? Brent was a good man, he was not just any man. My emotions would shoot up again. Everything will be fine, I'd think. We're still alive, and where there's life there's hope. Then I'd feel happy again – sometimes wildly happy; the way I'd feel whenever one of his letters came and I'd be aware of everyone watching me, because that kind of happiness was impossible to hide.

From the start I knew Aza was something special. Even without being able to speak her language, I could tell that she had an incredible heart and soul. Very soon I was totally smitten and my whole life revolved around spending time with her, even though it was never just the two of us. There was always someone with her – her grandmother, her little sister or her brother, her mother, her father.

It really hurt me to see her rotting away in that place, because that's all those people were doing, just rotting away.

Here was a woman who'd had everything in life; she had her university studies, she had a job, she had independence. She had *normality*. She was living the way people all over the world expect to be able to live. Suddenly it had all been stripped from her, and now she was trapped in this desperate hole, maybe until she died. It was as if she'd been locked in some stinking jail and the key thrown away. It wasn't a life; these people were barely surviving. Most of the time they didn't know where their next meal was coming from. It was just a matter of getting through one day and then, maybe, the next. Many of them didn't care whether they lived or died; there wasn't much difference as far as they were concerned.

I still think about what they were going through and how they were living. I think about Bosnia every day of my life – about something we did or something that happened. You can't help but do so.

One day, when we were bringing supplies back from Sarajevo, my colleague and friend Jos found some rotten bananas in the trailer. He threw them away, and suddenly all the children who used to trail round after us were screaming and scrambling for these bananas. They were fighting to grab a squashed, brown piece of fruit.

I stood back and looked. I have cousins the same age as those children. I thought, 'What if this happened to them?' Funny how small things can suddenly affect you so profoundly.

Maybe I got too involved, too personal. I think it was because I'd had such a fortunate life that it affected me more than some of the others. Or perhaps they were just better at shutting it all out.

It's possible to give things too much thought. You could spend a lifetime asking 'Why?' but it has happened. There has been enormous suffering and pain. The rest is for the history books.

Part 1

Aza

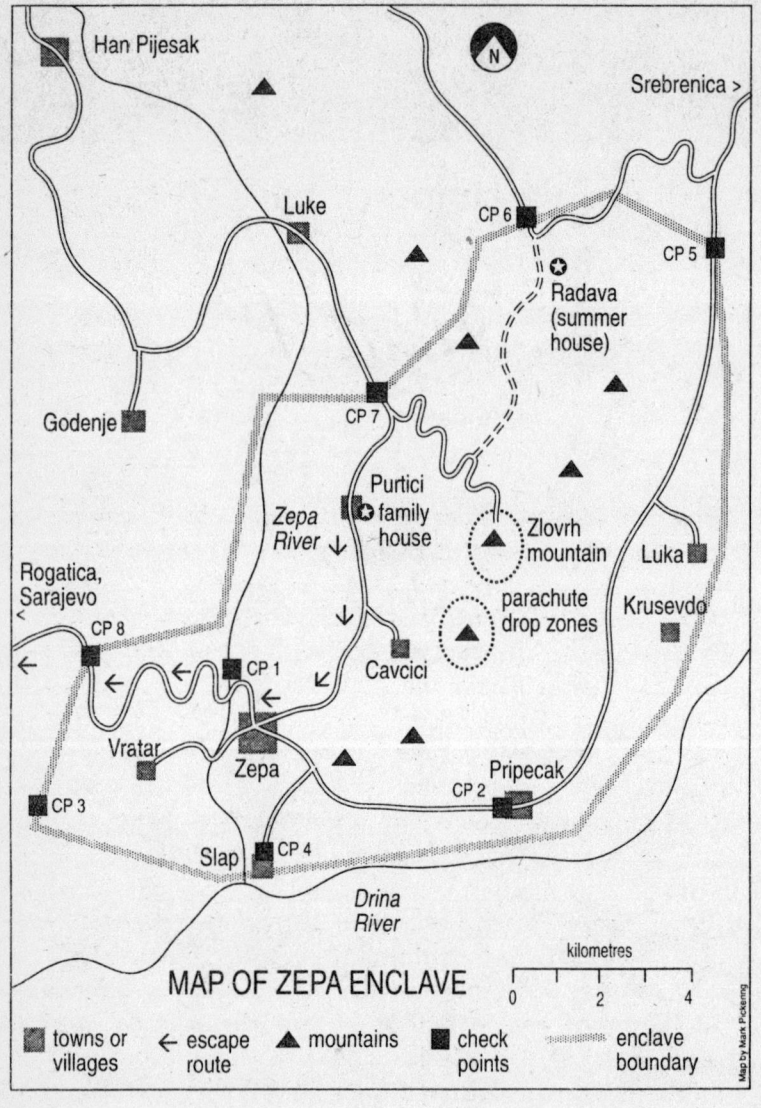

chapter one

Spring, 1992

How can I see our lives before the war? How I can see my village? I see that it is springtime and summertime, the whole place nice and quiet. You can see old trees with green leaves on top and all blossom underneath. And there is grass everywhere, and yellow and white flowers. You can hear the birds up in the tree next to you; it is an apple blossom tree. And all the bees. It is just like a beautiful garden because everything is growing, everything is so young.

Then it's war. You try to be very brave.

But our village was beautiful, just beautiful.

When I was young I had two brothers – one older and the other a year younger than me. We had our parents and grandparents – that is, my mother's father and mother, Nazif and Muška. Also we had an aunt, my mother's younger sister, Osmana, who was deaf and dumb, and she lived with us.

My father, Mustafa Mehmedovic, came from a big family, and when he was going to marry my mother, Sulejmana, my grandparents said, 'Come and live with us, because we don't have a son and your father has plenty of sons and daughters.' So my father came and they treated him just like a son.

Our house, which was built just after the Second World War, was big for that time: it had two bedrooms, a lounge, a kitchen, a bathroom and a pantry. But we needed it to be even bigger, so when I was about three years old we added another three bedrooms. We were able to enlarge the house at that time because my father had a job that allowed him to come home every night. He drove large trucks and this meant that sometimes he'd be away for a long time, working in another country. Because of this, when I was just a tiny girl, I didn't know what my father looked like.

Back then, when I was little, I slept in the same room as my younger brother, Hamdija. He and I were like twins. For about eight years we went to school together, while my older brother, Alija, travelled on a bus to another school in a bigger village. Hamdija and I didn't like the children from our big brother's school; they seemed a wild lot.

There was no bus to our school because it wasn't that far – only five kilometres each way. The walk was good exercise and we just accepted it, reasoning, 'Our village is in the middle of the whole of Yugoslavia, so it's too far away to be important. Buses are for people who work. You can't have buses for everyone!'

So we walked to school for many years, though in the winter it could be hard. Sometimes it would snow, and there you would be, just little, with your lunch and books in a big bag on your back. Going from home to school was downhill, but from school to home it was all up, up, up. Sometimes you would be very late getting home because you'd stopped too often, finding things on the road, or daydreaming and looking around you. When you were very small that was acceptable, but when you got older there were tasks that had to be done when you got home, so all the time you'd be nagging the younger ones, 'Come on!'

Because of having to walk, we didn't start school until we were six or seven. Then, after eight years of walking to school and back with my brother, I started at high school. This school was in another town and I had to leave home just after five o'clock in the morning to catch the bus. Every day I would pack my bag and go, but I always left on my own because my younger brother decided that he would rather stay home than go on to high school. Living in a village means that life at home is interesting and you always have plenty to do. So Hamdija stayed home and drove a big tractor and passed the time with his friends. He had many friends, young and old, because he was always helping somebody.

Then one day, when I arrived home from school, Hamdija's friends came to tell us that he'd had an accident with the tractor. It had rolled over a few times but he was alive, they said, it was nothing serious. For about four hours he was talking and walking, but he had blood in his ears and in his nose. They took him to the hospital in Sarajevo where he went into a coma and seven days later he died. He was fifteen years old. Two hours before his death my father called the hospital to ask how my brother was and the doctor told him that everything was all right.

On that same day, just before we learned that my brother was dead, a girl in the village hanged herself, maybe at the very moment that Hamdija died. She was one year younger than him and she had the same name. It was pronounced a little differently, because one was a girl's name and one a boy's, but it had the same meaning.

Nobody ever found why she did it. She had a good family, an older sister with whom she went to school. Her mother was out looking after sheep on the mountain when the girl was found. When she was told what had happened, the woman began to cry and walk about in a way that made your hair stand on end. Back in the house the mother began to destroy everything; she was out of her mind with sorrow.

Soon after that we discovered that my brother was dead, so the funeral was for both of them. Hundreds and hundreds of people came. My friends from high school, his friends, and hers from school, a busload of my father's family who lived in another town, all our friends. Nobody went to work that day.

After the funeral my older brother and I felt, deep inside us, that something was missing in our lives, and we asked our mother to have a baby for us. She said, 'I can't. I'm too old. There would be at least sixteen years between you. And what would people say?'

We begged her. 'We don't care about that. Oh, please? Please?'

She said, 'Maybe it won't be a boy.'

'We don't care.'

Within two years my mother was expecting another baby, but there were problems: she had toxaemia, and had to spend the last months in hospital. At home that left me, my father and my grandmother. Most of the time, my aunt stayed at our summer house in the mountains with my grandfather. Every spring my grandfather took his sheep into the mountains so the land in our village could be planted for crops, and grass grown for hay, and my aunt would go to help him and do the cooking.

My father would be away at work, but my grandmother was always at home. There was a lot to do: we had an orchard and a garden, as well as sheep and hens and three or four cows. My grandmother was only perhaps sixty, but her life had been hard and she couldn't do very much. I was away twelve hours each day at school, then coming home every night to do the cooking, washing and ironing. Then, in the weekend, because it was spring, I was planting and watering in the garden. It was hard, and I was worried about my mother: although she wasn't old, she had been through much, especially my brother's death. But, always, there was the thought of that little baby to look forward to.

Finally my little sister was born, a caesarean birth because, at the last moment, the doctor told my mother that the baby's cord was around her neck and my sister must be born at once or she would die.

I was at home in my bedroom upstairs when my father arrived with the news of the baby. My grandmother came into my room and she was crying.

I said, 'What? What?'

'You have a little sister.'

I was so happy that I cried too. I had been sure this baby would be a boy – I think we all expected that – but I didn't care. She must, I thought, be called Alida.

I went with my father to visit Majka, but we weren't allowed into her room because she wasn't well enough. Even my father, when he visited, was only allowed to see her from the window. Not knowing how long she would be in hospital, we were all very worried about her.

The hospital system in Sarajevo was not good. The nurses would sit around drinking coffee, talking and smoking, and would take no notice if their patients were calling for help. My mother, we learned later, had a fit of coughing in the night and her stitches broke, but no one did anything until the morning. She came close to dying and when the doctor found out what had happened, he was extremely angry. So they put in more stitches, and then more after that.

My little sister had stayed in the hospital, but my mother became too ill to breastfeed her. And then we discovered that the baby had a thyroid problem that could prevent her body from growing normally, and some tests were needed. So both my sister and my mother stayed in hospital, and I was thinking, 'Oh please, let my Majka be all right – it doesn't matter so much about the baby.'

We began going to the hospital to help feed Alida and take her home for weekends. She was such a tiny thing. My father and I would take her in the car and I would look into her carry-cot every five seconds, and she would be watching me with her dark eyes. When she fell asleep, I would hold her against me, never moving my arms all the way home, which was a two-hour journey over rough roads.

Eventually they both came home, but my mother was not well, and had to go back to the hospital many times. She was too weak and ill to look after my sister, so much of the time this was my job. In the evenings I would wash the nappies for my grandmother to use the next day, and at night, if my sister cried, I would go to her. When she had a cold or was distressed, she would cry to be held, and as soon as I put her down she would begin to cry again. Many nights I got no sleep at all.

I was seventeen then, and still going to high school. Every day I was seeing my sister grow and feeling how much I loved her. It was as if she were my own child.

When my young brother had been killed, I had taken it so hard that I had raged at God. 'Why did you do this to me? You've taken away the best thing that ever happened to me in my whole life.' Hamdija had been my soulmate; he'd meant everything to me.

But then God gave me my little sister, for whom I would give my life. He gave me somebody whom I could love as much as, maybe even more than, I had loved my brother. That seems a terrible thing to say, but this time I felt that God had given me someone whom I would be able to love for the rest of my life.

After Hamdija died I would cry myself to sleep, and then one night my younger brother came to me. He was right there in my room.

'You're dead,' I told him.

'No, I'm not. I'm alive.'

'Oh, this is just a dream.' I pinched myself, in order to wake up, but I was already awake. 'You really are alive!' I was filled with happiness. We were together; Hamdija was with me. Then it was as if I were waking up and he was no longer there.

I believe that moment with my brother was God's way of telling me that he was sorry, and that I mustn't grieve any longer.

In Purtići, the village where I lived, there were about twenty houses. In five minutes you could walk over the hill to the next village and pass two or three houses on the way. Each village had a name. Some were bigger and some were smaller – a thirty-minute walk from Purtići, for example, would bring you to a village with a hundred houses. The villages were all part of Zepa, but separate too, like suburbs.

Living there, you knew everyone in your area and everyone knew you. If you had a problem, everyone knew about it. If you were happy, everyone knew you were happy; if you were sad, everyone knew that too. If you had something to celebrate, there was no need to invite people – they just arrived. They would come not necessarily all together or on a particular day; for that whole month you might have different people arriving each day. You would need to have enough food for them all, although many people wouldn't eat because they knew you were too busy to be preparing food. These visitors were your guests; they neither brought food nor helped. But all your neighbours would have full cupboards because they would know that these people were coming to your place and needed to be fed. Even your relations, when they visited, were your guests. They sat; they did not bring food, they did not do dishes. To do so would have been most impolite. In winter there wasn't much to do so people would visit their relations, just for the company, and if you were the guest you would sit and be looked after.

But in the fields, and when there were things that needed to be done, everybody helped each other. And if people had more than they needed, maybe from their gardens, they gave it away. Some families had a little more than others but no one was really rich and it wasn't usual to make comparisons. It was not 'I am richer than you', but 'Can I can help you in some way?' Life was good.

Like us, many people from the villages had summer houses in the mountains where they would graze their animals in spring. We children would spend our summer holidays up there, and it was always great fun. Everyone would work together, drink together, eat together. One day you'd work for your neighbour and the next day he'd work for you. Fifty people scything the long grass could have it finished in two or three hours and, if we used a machine, the hay was made even faster. Sometimes we would work long hours and become very tired, but that did not matter because we were with friends. We would laugh and talk and sometimes hug one another. That's how it was.

But winters on the mountain were terrible, although, as a child, I could only imagine how cold they might be. I knew that we couldn't keep our cows on the mountain during the winter because they would be frozen, and that sometimes when there was a hard frost the trees in the forest would crack like gunfire as their sap froze and snapped. I remember, one day at school, being told that the temperature on the mountain had caused the barometer to break at minus thirty-seven degrees.

Often, when it was raining in our village, snow would be falling on the mountain above. The village was about eight hundred metres above sea level, while our summer house – right up the top of the mountain – was about fifteen hundred metres high.

I was fourteen when I began high school in Han Pijesak, which wasn't far away but the journey took about an hour on the bus. At school if you didn't pass the exams you had to stay another year in the same class, and then, perhaps, even the year after that. This meant that you could have friends in your class who were perhaps two years older than you, but it was hard on those older children to be with all the younger ones. Everyone tried to help those older ones as much as they could.

Under our communist system, religious teaching was not allowed in the schools. But some of the more traditional families wanted their children to have religious instruction, so those children would take time off school and the teachers would more or less turn a blind eye.

Zepa was a Muslim area and the children at our primary school came from Muslim families. Only a few were strict Muslims who attended the mosque regularly, but most people in Zepa would go at least four or five times a year on the important days of the Muslim calendar. And the whole community would share the same special holidays and celebrations in the way that Christians celebrate Christmas and Easter.

Although my grandmother was a fairly devout Muslim, my parents weren't strict about such things. There was an old man who taught religious instruction to some of the local children but our parents left it up to us to decide whether we would go to his classes. My mother believed that it was a good thing to know about, even if we didn't wish to practise it. But being Muslim didn't mean much to me; I was a communist first and foremost.

All the same, when I was about twelve I decided I would go along to that old man's classes with some of my girlfriends. They were held in the mosque, and on the day that I turned up there were about a dozen of us there. I'd only just arrived and I was chattering to one of my friends. Whatever she said made me laugh, and when I did the old man turned me out of his class. I was furious. *You think I'll be back, but I'll show you. You will never see me again!*

Han Pijesak was a Serb area. The Serb religion, Orthodox, was not very different from Catholicism – which was perhaps why the two groups didn't get along. For Serbs, almost every second day had some special religious significance, but some days – in fact five in a row – were particularly important and you weren't allowed to do anything at all. I would have hated that.

At high school, all my girlfriends were Serbs and I would often stay in their homes, which weren't much different from my own. In autumn, their families and many other Serbs would come to buy plums from us in Zepa. We had the best plum-growing climate in east

Bosnia and the Serbs would buy many plums and turn them into *rakija*, a domestic brandy made out of fruit. Most of my father's and brother's friends and my own were Serbs. They would come to our home and drink with us; you couldn't see or feel any difference between us.

We knew, as children, that the Muslims and Serbs had been enemies in the Second World War, but my grandfather had fought in that war and he never told me that I must stay away from Serbs. His neighbour on the mountain was a Serb and, although they had fought on opposite sides in the war, now they were friends. The feeling among our people was that although it was acceptable to be good friends with Serbs, it wasn't good to marry one. If a Serb and a Muslim married, the reasoning went, what about their children? 'I don't want my grandchild to be half and half.' That feeling was widespread and deeply entrenched.

I was never ashamed of being Muslim, but I couldn't see that it had much to do with who and what I was as a person. So at high school, once I saw how some people reacted to the name Mehmedovic, I began sometimes to call myself by other, Serb, names. I was to do the same when I went on to university.

My boyfriend at high school was Serb, but my family never knew about that. Some of them perhaps guessed, but I was glad that no one told my father. There were people in our village who would have given my family a hard time over something like that. When this boy and I parted company, I didn't have any more boyfriends at all because I didn't want my family to suffer. But I didn't see my high school friends as being different from me because they were Serb, and they never regarded me as being different from them. We went everywhere together; we were good to one another.

In my family we also were friends with some Catholics – that is, Croats, for Croatia is a Catholic area. For many years after 1945 everyone – Croats, Muslims, Serbs – had lived alongside one another like brothers and sisters, but over time the Croats and the Serbs had ceased to be friends.

Those of us who stayed on at high school were there until we were nineteen or twenty years old. And for all the boys, when they reached that age, there was compulsory military training. They had to serve in the army for a whole year and, after that, they were in the reserve forces until they turned twenty-seven. And all the girls between seventeen and nineteen had to practise with guns.

We learned about all types of guns, so I was familiar with every kind of weapon the Yugoslav army owned. I could, in two or three minutes, dismantle any one of them and put it back together. I was almost always better at this than the boys. We also had shooting practice with real guns. For a whole year we learned to shoot. If you were no good, you had to do it all over again. Luckily I was a crack shot.

It was necessary to protect our country; our history showed us that. We were so badly damaged by the Germans and others in the Second World War. We believed we had to protect our country, but we didn't know who from. Germany? Austria? Bulgaria? Hungary? They all seemed to be our friends, but you could never be sure. Serbia was our nearest neighbour, our closest friend!

The boys who went off to do their army training were Serb, Muslim and Catholic, all of them together and all thinking they were on the same side. And everybody who worked – the whole country – paid ten per cent of their earnings to the military. For medical costs, we paid only two per cent of our earnings; the army got the biggest amount by far. The army officers were paid good money and had the best houses, but we didn't mind. We remembered the war and believed we were building an army that would ensure such suffering would never happen again. We were doing this together. What's mine, we said, is yours.

After they finished at high school many of my girlfriends decided to take a job and get married, but I was an independent thinker and I wanted to go to university. I knew this would be hard for my family, because the university was a long way from our village and because there was so much to do at home.

At first my parents thought no, as did my grandmother, because she would miss me so much. But my grandfather wanted me to know everything. I did very well at high school so he was happy for me to go to university. And then, when he saw that there was no more for me to learn at high school, my father changed his mind and decided yes, I should go. So in 1991 I left all my close friends and went to the university in Sarajevo to study botany, forestry and horticulture. I was nineteen.

It was hard. I stayed at my aunt's place while her husband was away working in Belgrade, but I couldn't read or study there because her three children were always jumping around me or over me. So I would go back home whenever I could.

I always seemed to be travelling; I would leave Sarajevo late in the afternoon and return on a bus that left at four in the morning. This was all right in the autumn but in winter, if there was a big snow, you could get stuck in one town or another – or even just somewhere on the road.

After a while I left my aunt's and went to board with

a woman whose husband owned a shop where both of them worked. Soon I started working there with them, just a little, part-time. This was a busy time in my life; I was meeting many people and making new friends. Once again, I would use different names for myself. At first this was so people wouldn't think of me as 'a Muslim girl', but then I began to do it just for fun. I would make up stories about who I was and where I came from and put on a different accent, and I was always believed. My boss, who would take calls for me when we were both working, would laugh. 'Who are you today? Who shall I say will ring them back?'

Although things sometimes got complicated, having many identities also made life easier. If I was with Serb friends who didn't like Muslims or Catholics, then I would be Serb. If I was with Catholic friends, I would be Catholic. I couldn't change the attitudes of these friends, I knew that. If I'd argued with them we would become enemies. If I let them think I was the same as them they'd feel comfortable with me and everything would be all right.

So I was making lots of new friends but I still kept in touch with my old friends from high school, and they remained my best friends. I had one very special friend, Slavica, who was three years younger than me, but we were almost as close as sisters.

Because I was in the city and living my own life, some people back in Zepa would tell stories about me to my family. They were like snakes, spitting with jealousy. There I was, a Muslim girl from the village, having so much freedom. 'She does what she likes!' That was the aspect that they couldn't tolerate. Most children in our village left school early, sometimes straight from primary school. The girls, especially, would stay at home to help their families. And, if they went somewhere, to a party, for instance, they would have a brother or some other family member to chaperone them. But I could go where I liked and go there alone, so they made up tales about me.

Yet my family really trusted me because they knew what I was like. I had no doubt that my father had confidence in me because, when I was at home, if there was something to be done he would ask for my opinion on how we should go about it. I was used to helping my grandfather and my father, doing all the boys' jobs. I was never scared of hard work. I liked gardening and I loved looking after our animals. My ambition, by going to university, was to have a big farm, with orchards, yet have enough money to pay someone to look after it.

Maybe that was why some people hated me, talked behind my back. 'She thinks she's better than we are.'

And I was always so nice to those people, giving them great big smiles and asking how they were, thinking, maybe, that this would make them feel bad. If this didn't work, then they could think what they liked; I couldn't stop them. If they had nothing better to think about, they were welcome to think about me.

Going to university was expensive, and my family was paying. Anything I wanted they would buy. We didn't have a lot of money in the bank, but we enjoyed a comfortable life. Among the Zepa villagers we would have been one of the most fortunate families, because my father was working and he earned enough for our food and clothes, and we also had our farm. Every year we would sell all our lambs, except maybe four or five, and sometimes calves because two or three cows were enough for us. All this would bring in extra money.

So I didn't need any money, but I was working at my landlady's shop more and more. Then I was given the chance to travel as a buyer. I wanted to take this opportunity, to get around and see other places, but I couldn't ask for my family's approval, as they would have said no, I must go and help them. So I just did it anyway. Since I didn't think my family would be pleased that I was earning this money, I couldn't spend it on my little sister, or any other family member. For myself, I could spend it on clothes, shoes and make-up – I could spend a zillion dollars on those things and still want more! – but really I had plenty of everything.

My friend Slavica was half Serb and half Catholic. Her father was dead; there was just her, her mother and her sister. They had very little money and, because they lived in a building where they couldn't have a garden, they had to pay for everything and life was hard for them. So I would give some of my extra money to my girlfriend's mother. She was Serb, but she said I was like a daughter to her. The first time I gave her some cash she didn't want to take it. She said, 'You need that money.'

'Not as much as you do,' I told her.

I said I would give her the money to pay the bills and she should use the money she had to buy something she wanted. She couldn't believe it. She cried.

That first year at university I passed all my exams and I went back for my second year in 1992. On the second day of the new year I broke my arm. On a beautiful day, friends and I drove to a mountain close to Sarajevo, and there, on the mountain top, I slipped and broke my arm. We had just arrived, and I hadn't even begun to ski; it was to have been my first skiing experience.

I broke only a little bone inside, but it took a long time to mend; I was supposed to have it in plaster for three months. I couldn't brush my teeth. I couldn't put on my make-up. I couldn't iron my clothes. It was terrible. But Slavica came and stayed to do these things for me. I was living in a hotel because I had been doing a lot of travelling for the shop and had plenty of money. That travelling was exhausting but I was always thinking, 'I'll just do one more trip.'

We stayed at the hotel for a month and a half, having a wonderful time. They had a casino downstairs; my girlfriend didn't like gambling, but I could stay there all night, just for the fun. I never made much money, but I didn't lose a lot either. It was the start of the year so there were no exams, and I was unable to write notes or essays because of my arm, so I just enjoyed myself. But I couldn't afford to keep living like that, and my arm was healing, so I took over a flat belonging to a family who had gone to Germany for five years and needed someone to look after their home. It was great. I expected to stay there for several months.

During my first year at university war had started slowly in Croatia, but I was busy and didn't have time to think about it. When my Serb friends told me we would have war I didn't believe them. It was out of the question; most of my friends were Serbs, my boss was a Serb.

Because our army had belonged to everybody, there were many Muslims among the troops, and some now found themselves fighting for different sides. They didn't understand what was happening. The officers said it was their duty to fight, to kill, and so they obeyed, but when they understood the situation many of them tried to leave. One of my friends from primary school, whom we thought was dead, came home with terrible stories about Muslim soldiers trying to leave the battle front and being shot, about others who had just 'disappeared', and about some who were still trapped at the front, afraid to leave or to try to let their families know what was happening.

My brother had already done his year in the army; he'd finished his service about six months before. The normal course of events was that he'd then be called back as a reserve. This meant, now, that he would be fighting against the Catholics, who wanted Croat independence. Fine. But why should my brother care? Why should he kill someone because they wanted to belong in a separate country?

I rang a friend who was an officer at the big army centre in Han Pijesak and asked him to find out if my brother was on the list to be called up. He rang me back saying yes, he was. They had already called my brother up but he had decided he didn't want to go. My officer friend, who was also my brother's friend, said that all the men from Zepa were refusing to go. He told me not to worry, my brother wouldn't have to go if he didn't want to.

The Muslim president, Alija Izetbegovic, then announced that Muslims should not have to fight, so the Serb president, Radovan Karadzic, said that if they did not get our men and boys, they would have to take all our fighting equipment. So the Serbs came to the enclave towns and villages and removed all the guns and gas masks – everything they could find.

By then there were Serb police controlling the roads in some of the enclave towns and villages. This prevented maybe half the Muslim people from going to those places but the rest of us would still go. I thought my Serb friends would always look after me. These police would check cars and buses, and sometimes they were very drunk and would take money or jewellery from the occupants. They knew that people wouldn't dare to complain.

On 27 March 1992 I went home to Purtići. My sister was turning four on 4 April, and 6 April is an important

Muslim holiday, with feasting and celebrations. I was going to stay for the week, then return to Sarajevo as I had oral and written exams coming up.

On the way home I stopped off at a mountain town where I had some close Serb friends, and went to have a coffee with them. One of them said to me, 'Please don't go into Zepa. There's going to be war there.'

I thought he was joking. 'Why should there be?'

'I can't tell you that,' he said. 'It's not my fault, it's not your fault, but there will definitely be fighting in Zepa, and very soon, so keep away from there. Leave Bosnia. If you don't have the money to leave, I'll give you money. Just go.'

'No,' I told him. 'I don't want to. I can't leave my family. I can't leave my little sister. I can't leave my friends.'

I was laughing, I really thought it was a joke. I said, 'If there's a war and I'm in Zepa with my family, will you kill me?'

'I would never kill you, or your family, but if the fighting starts, get well away from the road. Go into the forest and hide.'

You silly man, I thought.

So I went home. On 5 April there were big meetings and rallies in Sarajevo and after that all travel was stopped. I couldn't get back to the city, and people who travelled to work were told not to turn up. We could still walk to the nearest Serb town, where everyone was still working as if things were normal. It was very strange and hard to believe. We were like sheep locked in a yard. To be under someone's control in this way is a most horrible feeling, yet still we were sure that all would be well.

In the second week, people needed to pick up their pay, so it was decided that four or five buses would set out for Han Pijesak. My father, rather reluctantly, agreed to be one of the drivers, on the condition that his bus went last. They found that the road had been barricaded a few kilometres out of Han Pijesak. The bus passengers, who were told to get out and walk the twenty-eight kilometres home, told us later that the forest was full of Serb soldiers holding guns – there seemed to be one behind every tree. When my father saw what was happening he turned back. Those were the last buses to leave Zepa. Soon after they cut off our power supply.

By then we had heard that the Serbs had taken Višegrad, a border town, and we were trying to work out what we should do. Višegrad was a very long drive from Zepa, but by river it was not far at all and anyone who came to Zepa from Višegrad would usually come by boat.

But the people who came now were not in boats – they floated down the river tied to pieces of wood in the form of a cross, or just on their own. Dead bodies, about a hundred and fifty of them. Some had names attached to them like luggage labels. Some were so mutilated there was no way of knowing if they were male or female. A mother and her small child were roped together and put on a kind of raft so their bodies wouldn't just sink from sight. There was a woman's body with a long stick running from mouth to anus. Was that the means of her death or did it happen afterwards? How could we know?

I did not see these bodies, but I knew the people who pulled them from the river and buried them. There is no way to tell how it made us feel. You couldn't cry; it was too terrible for tears. You couldn't be angry; you were beyond anger. You simply tried not to think about it.

From that time we knew we could rely on nothing.

chapter two

Summer, 1992

I was crying, 'Why, why, why?' Always, you are asking the same question. But you can't find why.

We had been proud of our army. I don't know how to explain, but it was like you had this child, and you had fed him and done absolutely everything for him and then he turned round and said, 'You have fed me enough, I'm now big and strong so I will kill you.'

After we found the bodies in the river we knew that if they could do that to civilian women and children, they could do anything. At first I thought it must have been somebody with a sick brain, but I was soon to realise that there were more sick brains out there than normal ones, for every day things grew worse. Zepa was cut off from all other towns. We were just a tiny spot on a map over-run with Serbs. Refugees from other Muslim villages began arriving in Zepa. They had walked for perhaps seven hours, carrying a few possessions or sometimes nothing at all; when the Serb soldiers arrived at the door they had simply fled. Our houses were being filled with refugees yet we still hoped that everything would calm down, that we would be all right.

Then they cut off our power supply and we realised that we must do something to help ourselves. We had no electricity, we had no weapons, we had nothing. People began to make guns out of pieces of metal. It was primitive, as if we'd stepped back hundreds of years. Most of our petrol was being used for molotov cocktails and grenades. Others argued against all this, said it was dangerous and futile, but what else could we do? The Serbs might come at any time.

Up behind our house there was a large complex, much of it underground, which before the war had been the biggest army communications centre in Bosnia. We could see it from our vegetable garden, and there were always one or two people nearby. But one day there were many more people, and helicopters were flying very low, observing the terrain and recording places such as the caves on the Zepa riverbank, where people might think to run and hide. They were making maps, and when they left I presume they took all the staff from that army centre because we no longer saw people there.

I watched all this and pretended to be busy in the garden. You couldn't ask them what was going on. But as yet no one was shooting at us and we took hope from that.

At that time, my family was building a house on the mountain to replace our old summer house. They had started it the year before while I was at the university and they had all the building materials up there, which was lucky as you could no longer buy such things. So now they all went up to work on the house. They took all our animals except one cow and a couple of hens, and half our clothes and food, in case the Serbs came to our village. My mother, before she left, had also buried some food such as salt and sugar – furtively, in case neighbours saw her and dug it all up the next day.

For a month I stayed on my own at our house in Purtići and continued a normal daily life, looking after our large vegetable garden, the orchard, and the big new home that we'd built just a few years before. It was a lovely house with large rooms, and it had everything: TV, washing machine, freezer – all the mod cons except for a drier and dishwasher. These weren't much use to me now, but fortunately we also had a wood stove, to save on power in winter.

Not having electricity was frustrating. I was always having to light the stove to heat water, to clean myself, to wash clothes, even to make a cup of coffee. I couldn't stay up at night because the few candles we'd had were finished. We had fashioned some smelly little lamps that burned diesel but I didn't want to use those unless I really needed to.

One beautiful sunny morning I was doing some washing when my neighbour arrived to say that something was wrong because a woman from the next village had seen an army truck approaching.

I didn't want to believe it. I knew that woman. 'Take no notice,' I said. 'She exaggerates.'

He said, 'No, I think something's happening. Please just be careful.'

'I have to finish my washing,' I said.

I was hanging out the clothes when I heard a woman from our village calling her son. You could hear the fear in her voice, and the sound chilled me. I walked to where I could see the road that wound down into Zepa. A convoy of trucks and tanks, moving slowly. In half an hour they would be in the township. I thought, 'Oh my God, no!'

We knew from the stories of others what was going to happen. They were coming to claim Muslim territory, to empty our houses and take everything we owned. Everyone was running, spreading the news, putting more wood on the barricades we had built across the roads. There was no shouting or screaming; people were just quietly grabbing possessions from their houses.

I took two blankets from my bed and threw them outside, along with a woollen dress, not new but really nice, and I packed a few warm clothes into a bag (there were only cool clothes at the summer house) and threw that out also. I did not take much, however, because I was thinking of what I could carry and I knew that, if we had to escape from the mountain, I would be carrying my sister as well.

I decided quickly to make bread. Whatever might happen to me, at least I would have some bread. I thought I might not see my family for a long time. The Serbs might have gone up to the mountain too. I felt so alone. People were fleeing into the forest, just walking away and leaving their houses. But I wanted to stay and see what was going to happen. I heard gunfire, but it was far away.

I put my bread into the oven to cook slowly and lay down on the couch, still wearing my jacket and boots. Maybe an hour and a half later I woke to the sound of explosions; the ground was shaking. I had been sleeping through it. It wasn't Purtići they were shelling, but a village just over the hill. The Serbs had stopped at a barricade and were firing bullets and shells. The closest houses were hit and many bullets were going over my house.

I ran. I forgot about my bread. Outside the house I let the cow off her chain. Everyone else had left and I was alone in the village. When I was about a hundred metres from the house, big rockets began to fall; I thought they were aimed at me. I was so scared. Looking back, I saw smoke – somebody's house was on fire. I didn't know that it was ours.

I was running uphill, full of adrenalin. After about an hour I found some other villagers in the forest. Everyone was scared and full of disbelief that this could happen. It was dark when I reached the summer house, where my family was so happy to see me.

When he heard the shooting, my brother had left for the village, taking with him a gun he had bought from one of the refugees. My father had followed him. They were gone all night, and it had started to drizzle. I was worried about my brother, who had gone just in a shirt, and I was concerned about the cow, who was my favourite. We'd had her since I was little and now she was about seventeen years old. I wanted to go and get her but my mother said no, she would be all right, she had plenty of food down there.

My brother and father returned the next night and my mother was so glad to see them that she was laughing. I was in the bedroom and, through the wall, I heard my brother saying, 'Majka, you are laughing, yet our house has burned down.' I thought he was making some kind of joke. 'I don't care,' she replied. 'I'm just so happy to have you two back alive. Are you hungry?'

Our house and another three homes had been burnt. Later my mother cried about it, but I had no tears inside me. I felt empty; I had lost something I loved, but at least we were all still alive.

Down at the village the Serbs had been stopped by the very last barricade, which was a big pine tree felled across the road. Their tank got stuck on this and couldn't move forwards or backwards and, because the road was narrow, the other vehicles couldn't get past.

The Serbs were cutting at the tree and growing more and more angry, but still they couldn't free the tank. Luck, for a moment, was on our side. Next day when I went back to get the cow, I learned that a close friend's father had died. It was so hard to believe. Yesterday he was alive, today he was dead. The Serbs, unable to free the tank, had set fire to it, leaving an ugly, burnt-out monument. They abandoned other vehicles, too, that had got stuck. They passed through two villages on their way back. In the first, they set fire to the houses closest to the road; in the second village they burned everything.

On the road back to the mountain, I found my next-door neighbour, who was looking for her husband. No one had seen him. I said to her, 'Oh, he'll be all right. Don't worry.' But he wasn't all right. He was dead. They found him in a small clearing in the forest. Other people, refugee boys, were killed and some were shot but survived.

So we had stopped the Serbs this time, kept them from our village, but we knew they would try again. One of the vehicles they left behind contained documents, including a map in which Zepa was covered with a big black mark; they had also listed the Muslim holidays.

Now everyone was moving up into the mountains. In the area around our summer house there were thousands of people. Some had brought their animals with them, some were passing through on their way to the next mountain. Many people stayed in the forest, living under the trees.

There were twenty-eight people living in our still unfinished summer house, which had only a kitchen-cum-lounge, two bedrooms and a hallway – the bathroom had not yet been built. And our old summer house, which was even smaller, with just a kitchen-cum-lounge and one bedroom, housed about sixteen people. Next door to that was our cow barn, with a little hay loft; another three families were sleeping in there. We had another shed for the sheep, although it hadn't been used for the last couple of years, and some sixty people slept there. There were a few days of solid, heavy rain and people simply wanted somewhere dry.

Water was a problem. All our tank water was now kept for drinking and for washing and cooking we'd get water from the stream. Every day there would be a big queue of people waiting to cart water or wash in the stream. You would be washing yourself in the same water as the people beside you. It was hard. Everyone was thinking, 'What has happened to me? Last week I was living in a beautiful house with all my belongings, and now I am grubby and cold and I have nothing.' It was worst for those with children. The little ones wanted food all the time. What can I have? What is there to eat? I'm hungry. Their mothers would have to say, 'No, you can't have anything today.' Then tomorrow would come and the children would start asking again.

At first people seemed lost, but then they came to accept that this was really happening and they must try to make the best of it. Our first priority was food. There were no shops, there were no gardens. Some people had little bags of flour and other food, but there were many to feed. Our family had some sheep and the cows, and other people had cows, but all this milk went to the children.

Although it was dangerous to go down to our village in the daytime, because the Serbs had taken up a position close to Purtići, I made some trips to get vegetables and fruit from our garden and orchard. Then I began to go at night, which was safer. I went many times although my father grew very cross with me.

One night I went with some friends to their village, which was even closer to the Serb observation post. That was a terrible experience, because when we arrived there the Serbs were setting fire to the village. It was a clear night, and we watched one house burn, then another. There were still some animals down there and you could hear the cows and dogs as they burned to death. It was like a horror movie. Sitting there watching, I was thinking that perhaps my village would be next.

But we were alive, that was the important thing, and we must go on living. So I kept going back to our garden to ensure that my sister and my family wouldn't go hungry. It was a tiring journey. The road to the village was blocked in places with boulders and stones and often I would fall over. Once, when I'd gathered my green tomatoes and potatoes and young corn, the load was so heavy and I was so tired that I fell asleep in a garage beside the road. My parents were terribly worried.

Sometimes, when they knew that I was going, the children would want to come with me to get some fruit, and I would take them. When my father found out, he was angry. 'If one of them got killed, what would you tell the family?' But the children loved to surprise their mothers by bringing fresh fruit, and fruit was the only treat available. No sweets, no chocolate, nothing.

All the children on the mountain loved me, because if I had something nice I would give it to them rather than eat it myself. The refugee children would stand waiting for me to come outside, and wherever I went they wanted to go. It was the same for my little sister with her friends. She'd make friends one day and they would be her friends forever.

By the end of June there were, in our house, my little sister, my mother, my aunt, my grandparents and various other people. My father and brother were, by then, away at the front fighting. The mountain was full of refugees from the local villages because the forest and the lack of roads made it feel safer. Our already full house also became a gathering place for others who came to listen to the news on our radio. Everyone wanted to hear the radio – it was like a little sunny place in a dark forest, something in which you could trust, something that might bring you hope.

One night we had all listened to the evening news at seven o'clock and, as people were leaving, I was thinking, 'Good, now we can quickly have dinner', because there was not enough food for everyone. My mother and grandparents had gone out to say goodbye to the visitors and when I looked through the window I saw that those leaving had taken cover in our little woodshed. I asked my mother what was happening.

'Shhh,' she whispered. 'There are soldiers out there. You can see the green uniform.'

Green meant it was the uniform of our Yugoslav army, now taken over by the Serbs. I could see a soldier about five hundred metres away in an open, rolling field. I started to walk towards him.

'Please don't do that,' my mother said.

'Don't worry,' I told her. I had on my usual clothes, black trousers and black T-shirt. I liked black and wore it a lot; black clothes were considered a Serb thing. I walked towards the soldier and, when I got close to him, I felt rather sick because he had a big, heavy machine gun and at least one grenade. I said, 'Hello.'

He stopped walking and a big smile came over his face. 'Oh, hello. How are you? What are you doing here?'

I said, 'Oh, everyone has left the villages and become separated. I don't know what's happening, What are *you* doing here?'

'I left the line,' he said. 'I'm trying to find my way back.'

I told him he was heading the wrong way and we walked together for a while, before I asked him if he was hungry.

'I'm starving. I've had nothing to eat all day, just a drink of water.'

Thinking he knew me, he trusted me. Part of me felt so guilty, but my father and brother were out there fighting these people and I couldn't be sure they were still alive.

'Come with me to my place,' I said, 'and have something to eat, then I'll show you which way to go.' I took his gun. 'Let me carry this for you.'

I noticed that the weapon was rusty because of the rain, and that the barrel was dark from firing many bullets.

We walked towards our summer house where all the people were hiding and when we were quite close he saw the faces looking out and my mother coming foward, and he looked at me and his eyes were saying, 'You bitch!' Then he was surrounded and bombarded with questions. I said they should wait until he'd eaten, and my grandfather went inside and brought back a big piece of buttered bread, which he gave to the soldier. He was hungry, you could tell, but he couldn't swallow it, so my grandfather got him a glass of water to wash it down. Some people wanted to tie the man up but my grand father said no, because in the Second World War he had been tied up and he hated to see that being done to anyone or anything.

The man began to answer our questions. He told us, among other things, that he was unmarried. And then – I'll never forget this – Alida walked out of the house, cradling something, and walked up to the soldier. Everyone was looking at her, and we saw that she was holding another big piece of bread. 'I brought this for him,' she told us. 'I think he is very hungry.'

The soldier began to cry. He told us then that he was married and had two children. He was shaking so much that he couldn't finish the first piece of bread, so my grandfather told him to put the second piece in his pocket and keep it for later. You could see he was very scared. People were interrogating him about who wielded power in the Bosnian Serb army and the names he gave us were almost all people I knew. He would say a surname and I could give the first name. He was staring at me – how come I knew all this, yet was on the other side? My grandfather said the soldier should be taken to our militia's headquarters nearby, for interrogation by our commander. Before he walked away the soldier looked at me and said, 'Thank you.'

But the commander wasn't at the headquarters, so some other people questioned the Serb soldier. As they knew, earlier that day two or three other Serb soldiers had become separated from their group and some of our refugees had told them how to get back to where they wanted to go. An hour or two later those refugees had been shelled by the Serbs. So, after questioning the soldier, our people set off to take him to another house, closer to the forest. On the way, they said, he'd tried to run away and so they killed him. Maybe that was true, maybe it wasn't. It made me wish that when I first spoke to him, I had told him to turn and run as fast as he could.

It was hard to know how I really felt about that incident. Once you have met someone, it's much harder to kill them. My friends from high school were now killing each other, and they could kill me and I could kill them, just as long as we were not close enough to know for certain who it was. It is distance that makes war possible. It is much more difficult to kill someone if you are looking him in the eye. I deceived that man by letting him think that he knew me. I think I did the right thing, but it felt like betrayal.

In August the Serbs tried for the second time to take Zepa. We had, by then, our own Muslim militia – every male who wasn't too ill, too old or too young was in it. This time they came over the mountain and, after two days of non-stop shelling and shooting, our militia arrived with a truck full of guns and ammunition and the Serbs retreated, probably in a hurry, because they left some of their fighting gear behind.

My brother was in that battle and I was very worried about him. I was still on the mountain, trying to help my family and the other people there. My brother Alija came home with an extra gun, which he gave to me.

'Take this. I hope you won't need it, but maybe you will.'

The gun was for the protection of my family because my father was sometimes at the front and sometimes out scouting for the militia. So, after that I slept with the gun and kept it near me. It was hard to get used to carrying a weapon. Until then, the only things I was accustomed to keep with me were books or a handbag full of make-up.

After the Serbs left that time, everything went very quiet and I thought, 'Maybe it's over, maybe it's finished.' But it wasn't.

This time they came in planes. First they bombed near our village. We could hear the plane from the mountain: it went from flying normally to flying very slowly – that's a sound I can't forget. Then there was a crashing as the bombs dropped – they were cluster bombs, which are grenades enclosed in bombs – and then an explosion like the loudest thunder I had ever heard.

The next time the planes came over the mountain above our summer house. At about four o'clock one morning the ground started to shake as rockets began firing on us. We woke not knowing what to do or where to go. There was no safe place. My little sister started to cry, so I took her outside and we lay on the grass, my body over hers. I thought, if one of us were to be killed it should be me and not her. Everyone else lay on the ground too. After about ten minutes the rockets moved on to another place, and after a couple of hours they stopped altogether.

That day everyone went out looking for caves to hide in. My father, who had returned from the front, found a big hole in the ground and he made a wooden cover to put over it, and covered it with earth. It was at least a little safer than being out in the open.

The next time they tried to bomb our house. I was inside with my sister and another little girl who was three years old. Her mother had taken their baby down to the sheep shed to visit the refugees there. There was much sadness among those people; a few of the women had lost sons – one had lost both her sons, and she had no other children. What could you say? Only 'I'm sorry'. There were no other words.

When I heard the plane coming, I was expecting it to fly over, but it grew louder and nearer. I felt sick with fear. They must have seen our buildings and the washing on the line. The first bomb landed very close. The house shook as we lay on the floor. Thinking they were trying to hit the buildings, I took the two girls and ran outside, and it was as if there had been a huge fire; all one side of the forest was gone, leaving only big stones. My neighbour was beside me. I dropped down by one of the stones and lay across the girls.

There was a deafening noise as grenades came down. I felt something hit my back, something cold like a cube of ice. I thought I must have been shot. I tried to touch the spot but I couldn't feel anything. It was burning hot or freezing cold, I couldn't tell which. There was no blood. Little stones had landed everywhere; I was covered with them.

It was so quiet. The children didn't cry, didn't make a sound; they simply looked around with wide eyes. Getting up, I called to my neighbour, but she didn't answer. I thought, 'Oh my God, maybe she is dead.' I could see nothing but shattered rocks and dust. There was a smell of powdered stone. I called her again, and then I found her beneath a rock. She was crying and crying, and I thought she was injured, but she said no, she was just exhausted, it was all too much for her.

It must have been one big stone that hit me. Afterwards my back turned black with bruising and was sore for a month. It still hurts in hot weather. But at the time it was nothing; I was happy to be alive.

The noise of the plane was the worst part, and that has stayed with me ever since. It was so very close, and so very loud, and it came on you so quickly. There was no time to decide what you should do, and you didn't dare look up in case you saw something black coming for your head. You would be thinking, 'Please don't let it be me, let it be somebody not very nice.'

That was the first of nearly a month of air attacks, mostly about that same time in the morning. It might be rockets or shells. On impact, the shells made a disgusting noise, as if millions of glasses were being smashed all at once – only worse than that – and the ground would shake. The planes would come every day and then, for two or three days, there would be nothing, but all day and all night you would be waiting. Many people wanted to go – anywhere – but there was nowhere to go.

Over the time they were shelling our big packhorse couldn't eat, she was in such a constant state of fear. After a while she was nothing but skin and bone. And my big dog, Johnny, was always trying to hide beneath my knees. It was as if he were saying, 'I don't want to be alive.'

Nobody from our building was killed, but many people fled. The children were terrified, we all were, although I never admitted it. I knew that would have only given my mother something else to worry about. Everyone thought I was fearless because I was too young to value my own life.

The planes also used bullets and bombs. The bombs were as long as a sofa, and very heavy. None hit our buildings, but one landed just beside our house, in our garden. It didn't explode – the ground had just been dug over and was very soft – but it ploughed a hole three times its own size. The bullets cut into the trees so that, in places, the forest was white with damaged or dying trees. Once when a shell crashed in the forest close to a friend of ours, a big piece of wood embedded itself in his bum. His wife removed it and put alcohol on the wound because that was all there was. It wasn't funny at the time, but afterwards even he was laughing. People expected to be injured by flying metal, not by flying pieces of tree. When the shells exploded at close range just one metal fragment could kill you. If you were lying down it was safer, but your back felt so exposed. You would hear an explosion and be convinced that your back had been blown away. You felt like a big target, and you just wanted to be smaller, smaller, smaller.

The planes were the worst thing. From anything else you could run and maybe find a safe place, but you couldn't run from a plane. When the planes came it was like a bad dream where you need to run but your legs won't move. Especially with the cluster bombs and the big grenades, you didn't know where they were going, where they were coming from or when they would stop. Then, afterwards, you would sometimes see the plane zooming up and down, playing, doing aerobatics. The pilot was enjoying himself, maybe laughing: 'You people, you must be so afraid of me.'

You watched people changing, growing older very quickly. When the planes had gone, at first everyone would be babbling, 'Are you all right? Are you alive?'

Then they would all fall silent.

In September the Serb army made a fourth attempt to enter Zepa. This time, as we had been expecting, they again came over the mountain. For about four days our militia managed to hold back the Serbs on that one narrow, rocky road. This was our last hope of keeping them out; if they got through, our only chance of surviving was by fleeing to Srebrenica. Already my family, along with most of the people who had come to the mountain, had moved across to the next mountain.

I was alone at the summer house with my dog. It was the middle of the day, and I was exhausted. My head kept sinking down but, remembering what had happened the last time I was alone like this, I couldn't risk falling asleep. Then, hearing a noise, I took my gun and went outside.

The noise was coming from my neighbour's house

about two hundred metres away. She had brought her two hens to the mountain with her, and one was being attacked by a hawk. I could see the hen running through the bushes, trying to hide, and the hawk coming after her. He wanted to kill her, just as the Serb soldiers wanted to kill us. As the hawk landed on the fence, I fired and hit him. His feathers went everywhere and I thought he was dead, but suddenly he staggered off into the forest. I went looking for him but saw only some blood and feathers. Finding the poor hen crouching under a low bush, I tried to reassure her that she was safe.

As I was walking home I saw about ten people coming towards me, carrying someone on a stretcher. They were obviously heading for my place and I was thinking, 'Oh my God, who is it?' It could have been anyone because I knew my brother had been telling people that his sister was still at the house, and my grandfather had killed two sheep before he went, so there would be food there for everyone.

As they drew closer I saw that I knew one of the men, although not very well. He had six holes on each of his legs from a grenade or big mortar. I couldn't believe he was still walking. The holes weren't big but they were bleeding steadily.

The man on the stretcher had a bullet through his shoulders; it had gone through the left shoulder and into the right. He had to be my first patient. There were plenty of bandages in the house, because my grandparents and I had been gathering and saving them for an emergency like this. One of the men had a little bottle of *rakija*, and that strong liquor was probably the best disinfectant I could have had. I bandaged the man's shoulder, but this didn't stop the bleeding. His shirt and singlet were sodden with blood and my hands were red with it, right up to my elbows. I put on more bandages and cleaned him up.

While I was doing this, another three wounded men arrived. One of them, a very good friend of mine, must have taken a grenade. A big piece of metal had lodged in his leg, paralysing it, and his right arm had been torn off. It was just gone, and you could see bones, tendons, everything. I feel sick even thinking of it now, but at the time all I thought was, 'Quickly, quickly, get it bandaged!' I gave him some painkiller tablets we had saved. I was thinking, 'Oh God, make him go to sleep', when he lost consciousness.

Others came until there were wounded people lying everywhere. The carpet was covered in blood. The duvet where the man with the injured shoulders had lain for those first few seconds was a lake of blood. All up the walls there were bloody hand and fingerprints. I ran out of bandages but I found an old shirt of my grandfather's in the bedroom and I used that.

All the time I was worrying about my brother. Then someone told us that my brother's best friend, Fadil Turkovic, had been killed. Greatly respected, he was a good soldier, and everyone followed him. Hearing that he was gone we all felt as if that were the end; Fadil Turkovic was dead and we all were going to die. I was shaking, I was freezing, I was crying, and then Alija walked in, so I cried even more because he was alive. He was crying too. He said somebody must go to the mountain where our family was staying and tell my father to bring the chainsaw. Our soldiers had seized a truck but they couldn't drive it away because the road was barricaded.

Knowing that all the men were very tired, I said I would go. It was about an hour's walk, but I ran and arrived in twenty minutes, crying all the way. Nobody could believe I'd got there so quickly. I was trying to tell my father what had happened but I had no breath because I'd been running uphill. Everyone was looking at me. When I said Fadil was dead, they all went still and silent.

My father jumped up and went to start our truck, but some idiot had taken all the petrol. My father wasn't a man who swore but he was swearing then, because he needed to take the chainsaw to the men quickly and the truck would be the quickest and safest transport.

Instead we had to take our tractor. We had already wasted time trying to start the truck, so my father said I should go on ahead as I could run faster than the tractor, and could take shortcuts. This was true; I knew the area like the back of my hand. So I ran, and soon I heard a truck coming from another direction and thought maybe they'd managed to shift the barricade. I knew they would have put the dead men on that truck.

I was right. My father caught up with me, on our tractor, and we stopped the truck. I wanted to see the dead, I wanted to see our special soldier. Friends of mine were in charge of the truck so I climbed on. They said, 'Do you really want to see this?' I did. Fadil's left eye was still open, so somebody closed it. His body had been cut by heavy machine-gun fire. Beside him lay a boy who had been shot through his chin, arm and wrist.

Those on the truck told us that everyone was moving out, including our militia. Serb trucks were expected to roll in at any moment. People were leaving many things behind. One man had set fire to his little car; he couldn't take it with him and he didn't want the Serbs to find it.

When I returned to the empty house, it was just like a scene from a horror film. All the doors were open and there was blood spattered everywhere. You could see footprints through the blood and where there was carpet – it was a carpet patterned with red flowers – you couldn't tell what were flowers and what was blood. There was blood on the wooden walls, on the closed windows, on the couch, the chairs, the duvets. There was a puddle in one of the doorways that had already dried. A few flies were buzzing around. The smell was terrible. Or maybe it smelled so bad because I knew what had caused it. It was too much for me. I walked straight back out, and it was as if something inside me had broken.

I cried and screamed. There was nobody who could hear me. I had cried earlier that day because our special friend had died, but this was different. I was like a glass that had been filled with pain and now there was so much that it was overflowing. Up until that moment, I had believed that the war would end and that everything would go back to normal. But then I saw that things would only become worse. I could feel that knowledge collecting in my body, and it was more than I could cope with.

I thought of going back and burning the house down, because I didn't want the Serbs to have the pleasure. But that would have felt like another death. I had lost one home, but I still had this place.

That night they were to take the seven injured people to the Drina River and put them on a small boat to go to Srebrenica. That was the only way left to get them out. We wrapped them in sleeping bags and put them on the truck, and I held the man who had been shot in the arm because he couldn't lie down. We took them down our mountain and then another truck drove them to the river. All the way we were waiting for the Serbs to attack. Only later did we learn that they had decided to retreat at the same time as our militia. The boat left at three o'clock in the morning and I went to the next mountain to find the rest of my family, who were staying in a tiny two-roomed house with at least two other families. That night I slept lying on my father's legs, and wearing all my clothes – big jacket, boots, everything.

Next day everyone was preparing to leave just as soon as they had dug graves for Fadil Turkovic and the boy. There were hundreds of people on that mountain but they had very little to pack up, just what they could carry. Certain that the Serbs were already in the area, they were planning to walk through the forests to Srebrenica, the safe area. Hundreds had already left that same way. It was a twelve-hour walk over the mountains and at any moment you could be stopped, or killed. People would set off in convoy, reasoning that if something happened to half of the group, at least the other half might still get through.

Then the planes came. They weren't like our air force planes, they were a different shape, and we knew that they were going to drop bombs. They were combing the forests, and we were high on the mountain in a clear place. Oh God, they can't help but see us! I lay on my back, counting the planes. Everywhere people were lying and waiting, because there was no shelter. When I put my face very close to the ground, I heard what sounded like shells landing and trees crashing in the forest a little distance away. I lay there for about ten minutes and I felt nothing, but when the planes had gone and I stood up, I could feel pain in my face. It was full of prickles; I had been lying on thistles and I hadn't even known. Though the shells hadn't fallen very close to us, a few people were injured. Four sheep were killed, and a horse and foal.

When the bombing stopped our commandant arrived to tell us that the Serbs appeared to have retreated. In that case, I announced, I was going back to our summer house. He said no, because a patrol was still out getting more information.

'Yes,' I said. 'I'm going.'

'No, you won't,' he said. 'If I see you at that house, I will kill you myself.'

'I'm going.'

'Oh no, you're not. You will stay here. Even if I have to tie you up.'

I told him. 'You're not my brother. You're not my father. I'm not listening to you.'

He had no power to stop me. I could do whatever I wanted. Earlier that day I said to my brother: 'I don't want to leave this place, do you? Please don't go.' And my brother had told our parents that he and I didn't want to go to Srebrenica. Majka had said we were idiots, wanting to be the last ones to leave. Now I was so happy at the thought of staying. This was my ground. They could take me from my house but not from my land. I didn't want to be a refugee, living wherever they put me, surviving on handouts.

If the Serbs came now, they would go to the villages first; the mountains were the best place to be. So my family decided to stay where they were, waiting to see what would happen next, but I took my dog and went back to the summer house.

I washed everything. The weather was lovely, so I dragged the carpet outside on to the grass and soaked it and scrubbed it. I had begged from my mother a little of the soap powder that she had saved, and I boiled water on the fireplace (although I knew it was dangerous to light a fire) and I cleaned the walls and floors. I kept washing and washing, thinking I could still smell the blood. Eventually, the house was all nice and clean.

For the first three days my dog, Johnny, was like my shadow. When I went to fetch water, when I went to the toilet, which was outside, he was always with me. On the second day I found four or five potatoes so I lit a fire and cooked them up with a bit of dripping my mother had left and some salt I'd found in a cup. That was my lunch and dinner. I sat on the doorstep to eat it and Johnny sat in front of me. When I threw him a potato he ignored it, so I started feeding him from my potato, one bite for me, one for him. If I was eating it, then he would eat it.

I stayed at the summer house on my own with Johnny for nine days. I brought our animals back to their own pasture and in the morning and the evening I would go and see my family and take milk for the children of the families with whom they were sharing that tiny house. I was much better off in the summer house. At first people thought I was foolish – 'Why risk your life when you are still young?' – but then some began to say, 'If she can go back there, so can I.' They began to return to our mountain. On the ninth day my family returned.

chapter three

Winter, 1992-93

The frail, the old, the very young are the first to die. They say it is 'natural selection'. But no one will live forever, and I am always thinking, 'Why should I be the last one to die? That's not what I want.' Many times my family complained that I was never thinking about myself. I told them, 'Yes, I am thinking. I am thinking enough.'

Gradually those from Zepa who still had homes to return to began to move out of the forest, to leave the mountain and return to their villages. They didn't believe it was safe to go back, but the risk seemed a better option than living under trees or in rough improvised shelters. It was now autumn, which was always a time of endless drizzle, fog and cold.

Some of the people who had crossed the mountain to Srebrenica now also began to return. Their houses might have been damaged by fire or explosions, but

Zepa was still home, and they were happy to be going back. At the same time, others who were refugees and had nowhere to go were leaving for Srebrenica, where there were more people and therefore more houses, and where, possibly, they had relations or friends. Also, you could still get food in Srebrenica. Before the war it was a market gardening centre, exporting produce. And people could feel safer there, because it was a bigger territory with a stronger army. Crossing the mountains was still difficult and dangerous because of mines and Serb patrols – there were mines all through the forest – but many felt that they couldn't cope any longer with conditions on the mountain.

When my family returned to be with me in the summer house, they came with two other families, but most of the other people who had been in our building were now moving on. Our army tried to discourage people – especially those who owned guns – from leaving, but there was fear of another Serb attack. The Serb soldiers had an observation post overlooking Zepa so they always knew who was there and what was going on.

We couldn't go back to the village because our house had gone. All my father's family – his father, stepmother, sisters and brothers – lived in Srebrenica, so he thought that we should go there. We wouldn't be able to take our animals with us as there'd be nowhere to keep them. My grandfather had already told me he wanted to stay on the mountain, so I told my father that I would stay with my grandfather and look after the animals. If we needed to leave he and I could both walk to Srebrenica. I could tell that my father was relieved. He hadn't wanted to ask someone to stay, because if anything had happened to them he would have felt responsible.

So, in late September, my family set off with two of my cousins, who had been injured, and the other two families who were sharing our summer house. They went in the truck with all their gear and carried grenades in case of attack. My grandfather and I stayed behind with another woman who had two cows to look after. Her family had gone in the truck, although she thought her husband might return for both her and the cows. I suspected she was secretly glad to be away from her mother-in-law, who was hard to please.

Everyone reached Srebrenica safely and, within a week, my brother and the woman's husband, who were both in our militia, had returned to make the summer house their base, although they were almost always off on patrol or keeping watch. The army centre was only ten minutes away, and the soldiers were good to us. If they had fresh vegetables or sugar to spare they would bring me some, and I would give them milk.

Before they left, my parents had hidden grain for planting in the spring. There was a big plastic container, filled with about sixty kilograms of barley. After about a month we ran out of flour and my brother said he could go and get half the barley.

'No,' I said. 'Don't even think about it.' But the next minute *I* was thinking about it. 'Well, maybe...'

'Yes,' said Alija. 'We might not be alive next year.'

'You're right. Let's go.' But I thought, 'When Majka comes back she'll kill us!'

We took some of that barley and my brother went down to Zepa and got it ground by a man who had a watermill. We were terrible together, my brother and I; we had so much fun during that time. He had a girlfriend he'd met on the mountain, thanks to the war. Her name was Fatima and she was a refugee, now living in Srebrenica.

One night he said, 'If you scratch my back for thirty minutes I'll marry Fatima.'

'You idiot,' I told him. 'You can marry her if you want to, but I'll scratch your back because you're my brother.'

The woman who was staying with us had a house in Purtići and, as it began to grow colder on the mountain, she said we should move to her house. Then, some time in November, my father came back from Srebrenica, which meant Alija and I had to behave ourselves. My father said things were improving in Srebrenica. Didn't I want to go with him when he went back? I said no, I was thinking of moving to Zepa with this woman, to live in the downstairs part of her house which she didn't need. My father agreed and said he would come with me, but my grandfather opted to stay on the mountain. When we had cleaned up this woman's house my father said maybe our family should come back here and stay? The woman agreed – they could come as soon as they liked. But I wanted time to get everything nice, with the floors scrubbed and the walls whitewashed. I had brought some of our cows down to our barn, which was about a twenty-minute walk away, and each day I would go there to feed and milk them. The rest of the time I spent making the downstairs part of the house pleasant for my family.

On the night they were due to come we were told by some of our men that a big group of Muslim soldiers were waiting to escort our family, and the others who were travelling with them, across Serb territory. My father, very worried about the dangers of the journey, went to a neighbour's to listen to the news.

I was upstairs with the woman in whose house we were staying – she was very excited because her children were also returning – when we heard a knock on the door and a man's voice asking for Aza. I froze. Oh my

God, something's happened to them! That's how it was: you were constantly expecting bad news. As I walked slowly out to the hall, I thought, 'I know this man – he's one of our soldiers.'

He said, 'Aza, you now have a sister-in-law. Your brother is coming with his new wife, Fatima. They will be here in an hour.'

I couldn't believe it. One moment I had been frozen with dread, and now I was glowing with happiness. The last thing I'd been expecting was good news – we'd almost forgotten there was such a thing. In my country when you took someone as your husband or wife you could get married within two or three days at a registry office or anywhere. If you went with someone you were considered married, maybe not on paper, but as far as everyone else was concerned.

At last they arrived. It had been a very slow journey because there was no diesel so the truck was running on cooking oil, which burns very slowly, and it was carrying many people. My brother got out but first I was looking for my little sister. As I lifted her down and held her tight I was thinking, 'It's over. Everything is all right again.'

Everyone was hugging and kissing each other, and that went on all night. I said to Alija, 'Why didn't you tell me you were getting married? I could have made something special.' There was nothing extra to eat or drink, but we wanted to make it a celebration. And, over the next few days, we did. My aunt from Srebrenica had given us extra flour and my family had brought *rakija*.

The flour, kept in bags in a place outside, was going down fast. My mother said, 'We're using that flour very quickly.'

'Oh Majka, I know that,' I said, 'but I have to make bread.'

'Even so, it's going very quickly.'

She thought my brother might have been taking it to exchange for tobacco. 'Oh dear,' I thought, 'wait till she finds out about the barley seeds!'

Then a cake of soap went missing from a bag I had left in the upstairs bedroom that my brother and Fatima were using. It was toilet soap with a nice perfume. And, very early one morning, I came upon our friend – the woman who lived in the house – doing her washing with my soap. I was so upset. She had been living with us on the mountain for three or four months. We had shared everything we had with her and with her family. When I told my grandmother she was very angry.

Two or three days later two big pumpkins disappeared. Our cousin had brought us these and then they were gone. My grandmother went upstairs and found the woman and her family peeling pumpkins for themselves. They denied that they were ours.

Then, early the next morning, my mother went out to the toilet and found one of the woman's sons pinching our flour. He must have been taking some every morning. They had flour of their own, but it was only oat flour, which is darker; ours was barley flour. Majka came back inside with her cheeks very red. When she told us, I cried. It seemed that soon there would be nobody you could trust.

Next day my father decided that we would rebuild our house. Each day when I'd been going to milk our cows I'd hurried past the remains of our house, not really seeing it. Now I went with my father to look and it was such a sad feeling. I stood in the drizzling rain and remembered how the house used to be and realised how much I missed it.

The basement, which had been built of stone and mortar, was blackened but still partly standing. Our next-door neighbour, always a nice man, said we could have a bedroom in his house to sleep in while we were rebuilding, and that he would help us. So over the next few days my brother and I, with help from others, broke up stones with a pick and shovel and loaded them on to our truck. It was hard work. Then we mixed them with mortar to repair and line that broken basement and build a dividing wall so that it would make us a two-roomed house. But mortar takes a long time to dry and it was cold, with constant drizzling rain; usually our houses were built in spring so that they had the summer to dry out. We needed to get the roof on quickly.

We borrowed roofing iron from a friend who, before the war, had been planning to build a house and we went to the mountain to get wood. Everyone was helping because there was nothing else to do. So we built the roof, and for three nights my parents stayed there, keeping a fire burning to dry the walls. Then we moved in with everything we had, because we wanted to be out of that woman's house. You could still poke your finger into the walls or write things there because, especially at the bottom, they weren't at all dry. Soon our house was full of signatures and my father was saying, 'Oh lord, can't you people just stop doing that!'

We all slept on the floor because we had blankets and sleeping bags but no beds. We were given some bed ends, which looked nice, but there was nothing to go in the middle, so we joined them with floorboards and made mattresses from the curtains in my father's bus, which we then stuffed with hay. My brother and his new wife slept in our next-door neighbour's room. He said we must look upon that room as our own, because they didn't need it.

This was December, and the beginning of winter, so I was happy to be in our own place. It was a wonderful feeling. If you wanted to slam the door, you slammed the door. It was your house. And you could even choose which door to slam. We had two doors, both of which had been given to us. Our front door, out of an old house, had windows at the top, but no glass, so we'd wrapped it with plastic; the other door was the heaviest I had ever opened or shut.

At night, the dampness of the walls penetrated to your lungs. It was lucky my grandfather wasn't there, since he suffered from asthma and I don't think he would have survived. If you opened the window you could breathe easier, but you risked dying of cold. I was constantly worried about my little sister; she was so tiny and I was afraid she might stop breathing in the night.

We had heard on the news that the United Nations had said the aerial bombing must stop, and for the most part it had. But the Serbs were still shooting from low-flying helicopters, and using small planes, of the type used for flight training or spraying, to drop large metal cylinders packed with nails and metal fragments plus explosives. With one of these they could destroy a large building or a whole big water tank. They had also dropped, just before winter, containers of petrol with explosives attached. These set fire to the forest so that people had to run for their lives.

As the air attacks came to an end, the machine-gun fire and shelling from the Serb observation posts began once again, more sporadically. We could see one of these Serb positions from Purtići. It was about thirty minutes away if you were to walk down into the valley, across the river, then up again, but looking straight across we were only about a kilometre apart. We could see them and they could see us. They watched us through binoculars. They knew everything we did. Sometimes we would shout across to each other. On traditional Serb holidays they would be yelling to us to come and have a drink with them, but we knew that, in a few hours, when they'd got themselves drunk, they were almost certain to start shooting at us.

We became adept at second-guessing what they would do. When it was raining they would put away their weapons, to avoid rust, so wet days were safer. On nights of heavy frost they might use their guns just to stop them seizing up. At such times we'd make sure that the children, and our neighbours' cats, were all inside. Alida thought it was good fun hiding in the house with all her friends. When the first shot was heard they would lie down with everyone else. They never whimpered or cried. Every day they would practise how to behave when under fire. It had become a part of their life. People were easier targets now that they had come down out of the forest and were hungry, cold and weary; and many, especially the old people, were killed by shells. I had a friend who had been a policeman in a Serb town. He died because he went outside on to his porch at the wrong moment and a shell exploded, killing him and one of his daughters and injuring another daughter.

The shelling and shooting finally stopped with the first snow. The weather must have proved too cold, wet and muddy. Still, we could never be sure that the Serbs wouldn't start again, so in the village or going to or from the mountain I was always very careful and ready to hide at any second. When I was walking I was constantly looking out for suitable trees, holes or rocks. You could never say, 'Today, today I am safe.'

But by then we had realised that we were more likely to die from hunger than from Serb weapons. By the time winter began we had already had about six months of war, and people had eaten all their food supplies. We might have grown enough in our gardens to store some away had it just been our own families we were feeding, but that food had been shared with several other families. No one had been too concerned about putting food aside for winter, because everyone had thought that the war would soon be over and, if it wasn't, they'd be in Srebrenica where there was still food. But that food was terribly expensive: a good gold ring or necklace would buy you just three or four kilograms of corn.

People were making the journey to Srebrenica in the hope of bringing back food. You had about a fifty-fifty chance of making it there and back alive. My girlfriend and her father were killed on a trip to get some corn, under cover of night, from a big commercial garden. Many mothers went off to get food from Srebrenica and never came back. If their husbands had already been killed, their relations, sometimes quite distant relations, would be left with the children, some of them little babies. One woman, who was left with a one-month-old infant, had no feeding bottle teats so she was using a finger from a glove. She was about fifty years old and the child was her distant cousin, but you could see that she loved it and would keep it as her own.

As the Serbs took over villages they would clean them out of food. They, too, were hungry, and sometimes they would be more interested in feeding themselves than in fighting. There was absolute confusion; people would fashion themselves large bags and pour into houses like locusts in the hope of finding food for their family. Our soldiers would enter houses and not know whether the people inside fighting over food were on our side or the other side. Civilians were arming themselves with improvised guns that were more likely to go off in their own faces than kill anyone else.

My family was very lucky because we had oats,

which were quite horrible but much better than nothing. The first time I ate the bread we made from oats – and by then we had no salt – I thought I'd just as soon die as live on that stuff. It was like eating gravel; you could feel it cutting your throat all the way down. Not having salt was terrible. I love salt. You could do without it on the table, but things cooked without salt were not so good. To eat meat cooked without any salt was like eating wood. Salt and flour were the things we craved most – salt and flour and tobacco.

Every day somebody came to our door asking if we could spare them some food, even just a little. By January we had about ten people asking each day. We often gave them silverbeet or swedes. Normally we fed those vegetables to the animals, but that winter people ate the lot. Also, we'd made a huge container full of what we called *raso,* which is sauerkraut, and we could give a little of that. And sometimes we could spare them milk. My mother would want to give milk to everyone.

'Aza, can you get these people a cup of milk?'

'Majka,' I'd tell her, 'cows can't give milk every two hours.'

The worst off were those who were already sick and on medication when the fighting began. Once they'd used up their prescription, they could get no more; they were dying. You would see them in their houses, looking like skeletons. There were two or three doctors still in the community but they had no medical supplies. It was very hard, too, for people with allergies. My cousin's youngest daughter, who was about four years old, could eat only cornflour; all other types of flour made her very ill. Her parents were exchanging the food they grew for even a small amount of cornflour. It didn't matter how much food you had, if your stomach couldn't digest it. Those of us who could eat anything were very lucky.

One day the daughter of the woman whose house we had left came looking for somewhere to live. She had a son and two daughters and her husband was an alcoholic (although not at that time because there was no alcohol), and her mother had refused to take them into her home, even though the basement of her house was still empty. I knew this woman and I liked her. When I used to come down from the mountain to collect vegetables she would come and help me, and I'd give her some vegetables in return.

They found another basement to live in, but they had no food, so every three or four days I would take a little bit of whatever we had, when no one was looking, and smuggle it to her under my jersey.

My mother grew suspicious. 'Don't you think of giving her our food. We have none to spare. Do you want to see your sister die?'

I denied I was giving the woman anything, but I kept on taking the food. And I gave her milk. I was the one who milked the cows so I could give milk to whomever I wanted and no one could object. I felt sorry for that woman for having such a mother. And I did the right thing, because afterwards the woman told her miserable mother that it was only thanks to me that the family hadn't starved, and that she never wanted to see her mother again. And by the time Majka found out what I'd done, she could only feel happy about it. We were all still alive and they were still alive, and the story of how I fed them would be handed down to their grandchildren and great-grandchildren.

But, more and more, people were thinking only of themselves and their immediate families. Villagers out searching for food were finding the frozen bodies of people who had been killed. There was no way of knowing who had killed them. Maybe it was someone who was after their food. Nobody tried very hard to find out what had happened. Everyone was too busy worrying about their own survival.

I felt so sorry for our poor cows. All of us had been so busy through summer that we hadn't cut enough hay for the animals. And then the war started and nobody thought of them and now they were starving.

My Johnny died during the winter. I had left him on the mountain with my grandfather, and he wasn't used to spending winter up there. It was a hungry winter for everyone, especially a dog, and when you are hungry you get very, very cold and you die. My brother and sister-in-law had been staying at the summer house and Alija turned up one evening just before dinner. I was very hungry and in a hurry to eat because I had many things to do. As soon as we'd set out the food and sat down my brother said to me, 'I have something to tell you.'

Everyone looked at him.

'Your dog is dead.'

He gave a little half-smile. I thought he was joking, but I saw my mother signalling to him, 'Don't tell her now!'

I cried and cried. I couldn't eat my dinner that night, or my breakfast next morning. I just wanted to go to the mountain to see the grave that my grandfather and sister-in-law had made for my dog.

It wasn't only hunger that made us feel so cold. That winter, with its heavy snowfalls, was the harshest we had ever experienced. We lived through it just waiting for spring to bring life and hope. When everything around us stirred into life so, perhaps, would we.

From the beginning of winter we knew from the radio news that the United Nations was trying to get food to us. We were so excited about this. For weeks we waited while the convoys tried to get into Zepa by various routes. When they didn't come we told ourselves, 'Maybe tomorrow.' That hope was the only thing keeping some people alive. Often we heard the trucks approaching the outskirts of Zepa, but there they were stopped, made to wait for a day or two and then turned back. We knew this was deliberate; the Serbs were taunting us, raising our hopes and then smashing them down.

The first convoy they let through arrived on a foggy morning just before New Year of 1993. I heard guns being fired, but in a celebratory kind of way, so I knew it must be the convoy. People were very happy; those trucks seemed like the best friends we had ever had, although no one got much food. As I remember, my family received, that time, two hundred grams of soya flour and a tiny can of pâté. 'Never mind,' we thought, 'more convoys will soon follow.' But the next one wasn't until February, just before my birthday. That food didn't go far either, but it was better than nothing.

Because the Serbs weren't letting the convoys through, there was now talk on the news of food being dropped to us by parachute, so we watched and waited every day. Never in my life had I listened to so much news. People would pack into our house for the news broadcasts, hoping to hear that the food was on its way.

With people living in crowded conditions, and little or no soap, there was an infestation of headlice. I had a horror of catching nits, so when the people left after listening to the news I'd be shaking out all our blankets and rugs. I thought nits could fly. When my mother asked what I was doing I explained and she laughed: 'They don't have wings.'

'Then how do they get from one head to another?'
'They walk.'

After that I imagined they were walking everywhere, but it was just too dark to see them. I would be searching through my sister's hair, poking and pointing.

'Majka, is that one? Is this?'

'No,' she'd say. 'No.'

My grandmother began asking me to look through her hair. She had long hair and, although there was no shampoo, she washed it every second day in hot water. She remembered having nits during the Second World War and couldn't bear to think that she might have them again.

I still hadn't seen a nit. Then, when she, my brother and I were waiting in a queue for the convoy food, my mother said, 'See that man in front of us? Can you see something in his hair?'

He was two or three people ahead of us. I looked but I couldn't see anything.

'Look really closely,' she said.

'Yes,' I said, 'I can see them. Now I know what they look like.'

Later, I met that man many times in the street but I couldn't even say hello to him. I would just see those nits and I'd keep on walking. I thought nits might take us over. There were millions of them and, even if you killed a hundred, there were a thousand more hatching at just that moment.

Soap and soap powder were precious. From the start of the war we had eked our soap out for as long as we could, but now it was well gone, and being without it was awful. How could you get your clothes clean? We found a way. You took ash from the grate, tied it in a piece of cotton, put it in very hot water with your clothes and scrubbed. Or alternatively you boiled the ash and water, left it to cool and the ash to settle, and then you used that water for your washing. After a few washes your white clothes turned a creamy yellow, so I usually used this method only for dark garments. The ash left a nice, fresh smell, but it was harsh like carbolic and peeled the skin from your fingers. It would have been risky to use it on baby clothes, so I don't know what people did when it came to washing nappies.

Everyone was strung out, surviving on their nerves, so life in our overcrowded homes was explosive with people yelling and fighting. It made you want to scream and escape. It might be your house, but it wouldn't feel like yours with so many people living there. But, because it was your house, you were expected to be responsible for getting things done. Often the others – your 'guests' – would just lie around, or go off to visit other refugee friends, and you would be fuming because it was left to you to clean the house or chop the wood. There were so many arguments that it was almost funny, like some absurd cartoon. You wanted to bang people's heads together. But underneath you would have the desperate feeling that you couldn't hold on for much longer.

Finally, the parachute drops began. We heard that a plane would be flying over Zepa and Srebrenica, but we weren't sure where the drop would be made. People went into the forest to wait in the hope of being first to find the food, but then our army made it clear that nobody was to pick the aid packets up except them; they would collect and distribute the food.

And they did collect it, but nobody got to see it. Word went around that those who found the food had hidden it away for themselves and their families. Everyone was saying, 'Oh, that's so rude. Next time I'll go myself.' So many people rushed off to wait for the second drop, but I held back, hoping the food would come at night so the army wouldn't see us searching. It was impossible to guess where the parachute would come down. If you waited on one mountain, you might see it land on the next and have to run for half an hour or more. In fact, this was to happen to me a few times. I would run my fastest but I always arrived too late.

The second drop came two or three days after the first, and then they came regularly right through into March, by which time they were coming every second night. The only way you could know where they'd landed was the loud cracking sound of the pallet hitting the ground. And when you heard that sound, you knew that if you were ever underneath it, you'd be squashed into pâté.

When you reached the pallet, there was more danger. People were desperate; they would be searching in groups, carrying knives for opening the pallets, and maybe guns – and people would steal those weapons from others if they got the chance. I usually went with another girl, my friend Nermina, and we would look out for each other. Sometimes knives would slash at your fingers when you reached for the food. Two girls were shot by a man spraying bullets to keep people back; one of them never regained the use of her legs. And these people were all on the same side!

My worst experience of the parachute drops was when a pallet landed in a large, deep, pit-like hole. I was with a group of friends and when we got to that hole and looked down, we saw a mass of people, about two hundred of them, fighting and shouting over the food.

I said to my friends that we should take only one pack each. Inside every pack there were two or three meals, each one just enough for one person. One of my friends gave me his pistol to look after while he was in the hole grabbing for food; he carried a pistol because a rifle was easily stolen at these food drops. I was on the edge of the hole, leaning down waiting for my friends to pass me a pack, when a man who had been running around muttering and cursing to himself suddenly produced a grenade and began waving it around. He was crazy with rage because he had missed out on the food packs.

'I'll kill you. I'll kill all you bastards,' he shouted above the clamour of fighting. Everyone fell silent. He was just a few metres from me. I knew this man; I went to school with his daughter, and their family were distant cousins of ours. He was holding the pin of the grenade. 'I'll pull this. I will.'

I raised the pistol that was in my hand. 'Move your finger and I'll shoot you.'

'You'll be dead,' he said. 'This grenade will kill you.'

'I don't care. You can kill us all but you'll die first.'

'This will kill you before you can kill me.'

'We'll see,' I said. My finger was on the trigger.

My friends were watching me, amazed. They thought I was going to shoot him. Everyone thought so. But I knew I wouldn't kill him; even if he threw the grenade I wouldn't kill him. I was capable of it, but I had decided not to.

Then he turned and walked away.

I saw that man many times after that. He came knocking on our door, but I wouldn't answer, I wouldn't speak to him. I hated him for his selfishness. He was the only person I thought of as my enemy.

Afterwards my friends asked, 'What if it had been one of us? Would you kill me, Aza?'

'Yes,' I'd tell them. 'It would be nothing to me, it would be as easy as drinking a glass of water.'

For the first few weeks of the parachute aid people would eat only a little and save the rest. They couldn't believe that the food would keep coming. Those food drops felt like a lottery win and you couldn't expect one of those every day. Children would lament about the delights they could be eating but which their parents had hidden away.

The humanitarian aid food came in the form of the little foil-packaged individual meals that soldiers get on active service. They differed depending on which country had provided them. The American life packets were pretty small and might contain ham and potatoes, as well as tiny portions of peanut butter or cream cheese and a piece of chocolate, a sweet biscuit or crackers and cheese. The cooked food often looked disgusting, but the taste was all right. There was one serving of coffee, sugar, salt and pepper. Also you got powdered cordial to make a colourful red or green drink, and chewing gum. That always pleased me; I like to chew gum.

The German life packets were a little bigger but we got fewer of them in a drop. They contained various kinds of goulash and portions of pâté or salami, and cheese, and *two* servings of coffee, and *four* little packets of sugar. Also, they had ten-pellet packets of chewing gum and a piece of very dark chocolate, plus a plastic bag for the freezer! The German life packets were great.

The Italians sent very strange packets. They came in shiny waterproof containers, and inside you'd find maybe a tin of fish that was actually eighty per cent oil and some pâté that I couldn't bring myself to taste, it looked so disgusting. There was, again, a piece of chocolate and something like jubes, but the best part was a small tin of condensed milk.

Once we received a packet that came from Thailand. Fish in sweet and sour sauce – delicious. But the French life packets were the best of all. They sent cans of food – sausages, fish – all of it beautifully cooked. We only had a French packet twice, which was perhaps fortunate, because a little of the French fare was just not enough.

When the parachutes kept on coming people stopped saving the food and, for the first time in two or three months, had enough to eat. The life package food was full of calories, and people who had been little more than skeletons now put on weight.

We had a middle-aged neighbour who, as far back as I could remember, had had a fat belly. But by that winter he'd become really skinny – just like an empty balloon – and his jerseys all hung down in the front. When the parachutes came, he began to blow up again as if the air was coming back into him. It was funny to see, but I felt sorry for him. He'd been a typical middle-class person, then the war came and one of his sons was killed and the other son, who was an air force pilot, disappeared. His daughters lived in other villages and both of their husbands were also killed. There was just him and his wife, whose health was very bad. They'd had no food, and no family to help them and he couldn't ask others for help because he couldn't give them anything in return. You only had to look at him to see all of those things written on his face.

Now that we all had some food, we began to visit our friends again. While people had been so hungry you didn't want to go visiting in case friends pressed you to eat food that you knew they needed for themselves. Of course, not everyone had thought like that. Some people, if they were really hungry, would come and sit around for the whole day in the hope that your family would eventually serve up a meal.

I remember one morning, before the parachutes started but after the second convoy, when I was cooking up salty pancakes to have with some feta cheese that we had got from the convoy. That was our breakfast and there would be enough left over to have a little bit for dinner that night. But, before we had even started to eat, a woman walked in. We had never seen her before in our lives. She went straight to the table and began to eat before we even had a chance to invite her. She ate and ate and ate. Big, hot pancakes topped with feta cheese. She was wolfing them down – who knows how long it must have been since she'd last eaten. Her hands were grubby and her nails were long, ragged and caked with dirt. After I'd seen those fingers I couldn't eat, though my mother was urging me to. I was just staring at this woman, with my eyes and mouth wide open. My father was watching me with a grin. I couldn't take my eyes away, and yet I felt so sorry for her.

After a while they included medicines in the drops and some people even received toothbrushes. Flour was what we needed most, yet they never dropped this – although it did come in the convoys. One day they dropped big bags of milk powder and people thought it was flour. I thought they were going to kill each other for it but when they found out it was milk they left it behind in disgust, because if they had cows they didn't need milk. So then I took some and, actually, it was good. I used to mix it in equal parts with flour to make savoury things.

Some people, especially the refugees, liked getting the parachutes almost as much as the food. They cut the fabric up and made skirts, shirts, trousers and jackets. There were little silky parts on the parachutes that looked rather like lace and some people would add this to their clothes as decoration. I thought it looked pretty ridiculous. At first I was quite keen to have some parachute clothing, but when everyone was wearing it I dismissed the idea. Food was much more important. And even though we sometimes laughed about what came down, the parachute drops were excellent; they saved our lives and they gave us hope.

But I was angry about the convoys. We had been so excited to hear they were coming, we had spent such a long time waiting, only to have about one every month get through. And even then, half of the aid would have been stolen on the way by the Bosnian Serbs, and things would be damaged. For instance, shoes that came on one of the convoys had been slashed to ribbons by the time they reached us.

If only the convoys had come regularly I could have stopped going after the parachutes. I'd had more than enough of waiting and searching in the mountains. I felt exhausted. Up there, chasing the aid drops, I would either be so hot from walking that the snow would be melting off me, or I'd be so cold that there was no feeling in my legs. It was just as if they'd been anaesthetised. I had only jeans, no long-johns, and the denim would be so stiff with ice that I would find, on taking my trousers off, that they had scratched my legs raw. I was so tired of all this. I just wanted a normal life.

But slowly, slowly, spring was coming and breathing life back into us. Grass was beginning to grow and you would see the hens out scratching for beetles. On sunny days I could shake out the blankets and leave the door open. It seemed that you could take deeper breaths. That spring, instead of always thinking about what would happen to us next, I just wanted to appreciate every second while I could.

In March, which was the first month of spring, the convoys came once again. And in spring, besides what we could grow in our gardens, people could gather wild plants. Stinging nettle, picked when it is small, is one of the nicest green vegetables you can have in soup or fritters. Another good eating plant was what we called wild silverbeet. People were gathering that as fast as it grew.

So, not only was it spring, but there was food to eat. After those months of hunger, having enough food was wonderful. It changed the way people looked, the way they moved, it changed everything. Having food was like seeing the sun coming out after a storm. Although, in fact, the storm was not yet over. As the weather improved the Serbs began shooting at us again.

My little sister and I were sleeping in the bedroom at our neighbour's house, which stood, exposed and alone, on a small hill. Our bedroom faced in the direction from which the machine-gun fire came and I would lie in bed imagining the bullets piercing the wall and then our heads. I kept rearranging Alida's sleeping position, her head this end and then that end, trying to work out which would be safer. On really cold nights, though, I would just take her into my bed to keep us both warm. We didn't have many blankets and there was no glass in the window, just cloth to cover it, so, when it was windy, the rain and snow would blow in. On those nights we would try to keep the blanket over our heads because, if you didn't, you could wake with hair that was frozen stiff.

On 5 May, when it was nearly summer, and most of my family was away staying on the mountain, I heard gunfire and saw some men and boys running around. I thought maybe another convoy had come in, since none had arrived since that one in March, but I knew we no longer had bullets to waste on celebrations, so I felt a little uneasy. Then a neighbour rushed in and told me to come and look from her place, which was closer to Zepa. From there I saw a cluster of houses and outbuildings with a haze around them.

'That's smoke,' she said.

'I think it's fog.' I desperately wanted it to be fog, although it looked too thick.

We heard more gunfire, and another house began to smoke. I went back to our house and told my grandmother, who was there with a neighbour and her two children. We were all saying, 'Oh my God, what will we do now? Where can we go?'

'I'm not going anywhere,' my grandmother said. 'I can't. My legs are too sore.'

We did not know it then, but at the first house that was set alight, the Serb soldiers had come in and killed twelve people by cutting their throats. Only one small boy had escaped the slaughter; he'd jumped out of the bedroom window and run.

We knew this time there was no way we could stop the Serb soldiers. So once again our people left their homes and fled into the forest, but my grandmother and I just watched them go.

Among all the thousands of people who had gone into the forest was a man who had a radio transmitter. He called a radio station in Sarajevo, asking for help. Without urgent intervention, he said, everyone in Zepa would be killed. Please help, he pleaded, and his words were heard all over the world, so from that moment everyone knew.

But what could they do? The United Nations asked the Serbs to stop, without success. Then NATO stepped in to negotiate. In Zepa the fighting and killing and burning went on right through those negotiations – and so did the parachute aid, although now the drops were made closer to the villages.

On the night of 8 May, when I was out searching for the aid drops, I found, for the first time and much to my delight, a bag of sugar. The next morning, as I was walking home with my sugar, the first UNPROFOR (United Nations Protection Force) vehicles passed me, and the Serbs had gone.

When that UNPROFOR convoy rolled in, people were at first fearful. They thought it could be a trick and that, at any moment, a bunch of Serb soldiers might leap from the back of those big trucks. When this didn't happen, such happiness broke out. Old women, crying and laughing, were kissing all the officers and telling them, 'You have saved my life.'

But all I felt at first was anger. I wanted to shout at them, 'You're late. What took you so long?'

chapter four

Summer, 1993

The UN soldiers really wanted to know, wanted to be friendly. They were always asking, 'How was it?' So you told them what happened on this day or that, and you could feel them thinking, 'Is it true?' Then I would ask myself why I was wasting my time and my voice. They could hear and feel how dangerous the war was, how cruel, but only when it was your own country and you were living there and feeling and seeing everything, could you really understand.

The arrival of UNPROFOR threw most of Zepa into a state of euphoric relief. The United States was given credit for saving our lives; everywhere people were offering thanks to God and President Clinton – he was our hero. Even I couldn't keep up my initial resentment for long. Better late than never, I decided.

For so long I had felt that the world must either not know the truth about what was happening to us, or simply not care. Otherwise, why would they not have stepped in to save us? Yet now I could understand why other countries might choose to hold back in the hope that we – the Serbs, Croats and Muslims – could sort things out between ourselves. If you see your neighbours fighting you don't feel that you ought to rush in right away. You think, 'It's none of my business', or, if you really care about them, you decide that, in the future, you'll try to help them to get along better. So you leave them to finish their fight and cool down a little, *then* you can try to help sort out the problem. I think it was like that for UNPROFOR. Unfortunately, when you are outside looking in, you have a very different view of things from those who are on the inside.

Not everyone in Zepa was happy to have the UNPROFOR observers. In return for UN protection we had traded our militia, and there were some who thought this was a bad deal. Even those of us who were glad to have the UN there did not have great confidence in what their presence would achieve. There was only a handful of observers in that first UNPROFOR team. How could we be sure that the Serb commanders would let them stay?

Then we learned that a whole company of Ukrainian soldiers – a hundred and twenty of them – were going to be stationed in the Zepa enclave. We greeted this news with mixed feelings; on the one hand the Ukrainians, who had close historical ties with the Serbs, were more likely to be allowed to stay and therefore stave off further Serb attacks; on the other hand, there was widespread distrust of the Ukrainians. And although a few of the Ukrainian soldiers turned out to be kind people who formed close friendships with the local people, the feeling of distrust was never dispelled. We were too aware of their close association with the Serbs ever to believe that the Ukrainians' motives were good ones.

One benefit we expected from the Ukrainian presence was that the humanitarian aid convoys would now be allowed through. We reasoned that the Serbs would at least want to ensure that their friends the Ukrainians didn't go hungry. But we were to discover that the Ukrainians had their own special resupply convoys, and while those got through, the aid convoys still, more often than not, didn't. Just as before, we would hear the trucks coming and we would be waiting, but at one checkpoint or another the Serbs would turn them back. Out of every ten convoys that tried to reach us, only two, perhaps, would get through.

The agreement was that we would hand all our weapons to the UN and, in return, we would become a UNpatrolled safe area, and no longer under Serb attack. So we gave up all our military weapons, but not the guns that were in private possession. There weren't many of these: out of some fifteen thousand citizens, fewer than a hundred people owned guns. Those who did wanted to keep them for their own protection; how could we know if the Serbs would keep their word or if the UN forces could be relied on?

In the same way that we kept back a few of our weapons, so the Serbs soon returned to shelling and shooting at us, although this was now sporadic and apparently mainly for their own entertainment. They liked to provoke the UN team, and would fire off a few rockets just for the pleasure of seeing the UN observers race to the checkpoints. Then they'd give the observers time to return to their headquarters before firing some more, to have the observers scuttling off again. The Serbs would be watching all this activity from up in the hills; you could almost hear them laughing.

Quite often, when the UN soldiers called at our place for coffee and a chat, the Serbs would start shelling near our house. One day I was sitting on our doorstep when the shelling began and the UN observer who was with me told me to get inside.

'No,' I said.

'Go on, inside.'

'No. Why should I? Have you gone inside? Then why should I? Don't tell me what I should do – I've had two years of this.'

I knew those shells weren't going to hit us. Over time you developed an instinct about when to duck or hide or lie down.

Even though our lives had improved a little with the UN presence, the unpredictable Serb fire was enough to keep us feeling constantly fearful and under threat. This was what they intended. Because we now had no militia, we couldn't return the fire; nor could the observers, who were unarmed. Our military protection was in the hands of the Ukrainians but, no matter how often we asked, they were not prepared to do battle with the Serbs and rout them from the surrounding hills. They seemed to find the very idea ridiculous.

To justify the continuing fire, the Serbs argued that we hadn't handed in all our weapons. They made outrageous claims about the amount of artillery we were supposed to have and demanded that these non-existent weapons should be produced. At one point one of our militia commanders took up a collection for money to buy and smuggle in some guns, which were then handed over in an effort to placate the Serbs, but it made no difference.

None of this was the UN's fault. I never felt, as some people did, that the UN observers were to blame. They were in a hopeless, impossible situation. They weren't allowed to take sides, no matter what they saw or thought. They could not change the big picture, but they did what they could. It was thanks to them that we now had food, and many of them regularly dipped into their own pockets to get us what we needed.

They felt so sorry for us. You would see it in their faces: 'Oh my God, you poor people!' I hated that; I didn't need their pity. Two years before I was probably living a better life than they were. Maybe everyone everywhere felt sorry for us. Why? Because the Serbs had kicked us around. But why did they do that? *Because we were stupid enough to let them*. Was that what those UN soldiers were thinking? Was it what I thought? I didn't know. I still don't know.

At first we regarded the military observers as curiosities. They kept their distance and so did we. If they came to our houses it was in an official way, to ask if we had seen outbreaks of firing or to talk about weapons and mines – which had the effect of making us feel more afraid than we had been before they arrived.

In spring many of the people who had spent the winter in the cramped homes of other families had moved back to live in the forest. Some had even left their own houses, anticipating correctly that with winter over, the Serbs would launch another attack. With so many people living in the forest, the makeshift toilet arrangements were in a disgusting state, and the smell was overwhelming.

Such things were a shock to the UN team when they first arrived. One British observer, visiting our house when rather drunk, told us off about it, as if we were children: 'There's really no excuse for living like that.' That same man saw our improvised candle – a small round food can filled with a mixture of diesel and oil, and a cotton wick – and couldn't believe it. It would explode, he said. The man was an idiot.

There were some black men from Kenya among those first observers. Our children, who had never seen a black person in real life, were wide-eyed, and if they got close enough they would stroke that black skin in amazement. The soldiers would laugh and hand out sweets, which were something most of these youngsters hadn't seen in a very long time. A few of the parachute packets had contained a lolly or two, but never enough.

One of these black soldiers, a man called Gabriel, would play with those children, cuddling and tickling them, and soon he was making friends everywhere. He'd visit people's homes, not just to talk about war but to drink coffee and chat about everyday things. We appreciated that. It was a long time since we'd talked with someone who had a normal life, and it was somehow reassuring – as if that normality might somehow brush off on to us.

It was as though Gabriel broke the ice, for after that our people and the UN soldiers began to feel more and more comfortable with each other, and would spend time talking, through their interpreters, about things other than the war. The downside of this was that, when you were with someone who, perhaps just ten days before, had been living a normal life in some normal country, it was very hard not to be reminded of all you were missing out on and feel sharp pangs of jealousy.

With UNPROFOR there our hope had returned, and so had some vestiges of life as we once knew it. There were vehicles on the roads again; admittedly these were mostly UNPROFOR or Ukrainian vehicles, but a few belonged to the local people. Our truck became a kind of taxi, transporting the old and the sick, or taking people into town to get food from the convoys. (The food was now stored and people were given certain days of the week on which they could come and collect their allocation.) And now our truck smelled, once again, as a truck should smell, of petrol. For many months we had been running it on used cooking oil; the parachute aid had been generous in providing cooking oil, but it wasn't much use if you had nothing to cook! People would store their old oil and use it as motor fuel. The way those trucks used to smell, you could have cooked pancakes on them.

My friend Denisa, who was also my relation, could speak English and she got a job with the UN observers as an interpreter. She would come, with the UN men, to our house. So I became good friends with some of the observers, and also with their other interpreters, Boriša and Miroslav. This soon started tongues wagging. People didn't believe that a young woman and man could just be friends – there had to be 'something going on'. These men would call around and I'd be there and so would half my family, but still those gossips couldn't accept that the observers had come just for coffee and talk.

I liked to talk. I enjoyed finding out about other people's lives, and telling them about mine, and I loved a good argument. To the mothers of Zepa's young men the thought that I might possibly become their daughter-in-law was a nightmare. Not only would I never have made a good farmer's wife, but I was also over-educated and argumentative. The gossip about me reached my father, who found it upsetting. Even though he knew it was nonsense, sometimes when I was going off to have coffee with my new friends he would protest.

'Go there, Aza, and you know what people are going to say!'

'Oh, not that again! They can say what they like. I don't care.'

In Zepa I was the black sheep among a white flock. I didn't mind being different, I knew there were plenty of people who liked me. But there were also those who thought that everyone ought to be just the same as them.

When the war began and I found myself trapped in Zepa I forgot my angry vow of years before, and began to attend classes at the mosque. It was the only source of learning that was available, and I knew so little about the Muslim religion that it seemed a good time to find out. I went, and soon I'd joined the choir. There were about fourteen of us and we sang in Arabic in the mosque. I enjoyed it, until one day the Muslim priest saw me sitting outside the restaurant in Zepa that had now become the UNMO (United Nations Military Observers) headquarters, drinking coffee with some of the men. The next time when I turned up to sing he started going on about my bad reputation.

'Okay,' I said. 'I don't want to get you into trouble. I'll leave the choir.'

'I'm sorry about this,' he said.

'Don't be sorry. If it's a choice, I'd rather be with them than you. They're just my friends, but I'll leave the choir, don't you worry.'

My girlfriend, Sabrina, was with me and she was outraged. She told that priest he was a bad-mannered hypocrite. He was shouting at her to leave and threatening to hit her, but still she went on telling him just what she thought of him. Soon after that she, too, left the choir.

I walked away from the rituals and the gatekeepers of religion, but I still believed in God. I always had. I believed absolutely that, over those past two years, he had been taking care of me. In the times of extreme fear or danger I had asked him for help, and had felt a response deep down in my heart.

Part 2

Brent

chapter five

Bosnia

I was in the fourth form when I decided that I wanted to be an air force pilot. I saw a British TV programme called *Fighter Pilot*, which was about men trying to get into the RAF. They followed one recruit who actually made it right through to become a fighter pilot. I thought, 'That looks like good fun!'

About the same time there was a seventh-former who'd left to join the air force, but he didn't get into pilot school. He'd been a prefect and quite a high achiever yet he'd failed. I knew then that it wasn't going to be easy, so I started taking steps to help me achieve my ambition. I took flying lessons, and went on a gliding camp. Also, a good friend of mine, Andrew Percy, who was a year ahead of me at school, was accepted into the air force and so was able to tell me about the selection process – what sort of questions they were liable to ask. That was a big help in preparing myself. I planned to go all out to get into the air force, but if that didn't happen my contingency plan was to go to university with all my friends.

I attended St Andrew's College, in Christchurch. My father, Colin, had left school when he was fifteen to do his apprenticeship in block laying. His brother became a school teacher but my Dad wanted to be out and doing. He was a hands-on sort of person, and that was probably just as well, because his father died not long afterwards, so they needed the money coming in. But my mother, Avis, and my father wanted to give my sister and me what Dad hadn't had – a really good education.

Not that a lack of education had held my father back. He's a very astute businessman with a strong will to succeed. When I started at St Andrew's in Standard Four his block-laying business was going well; he'd built up a successful company. But in the late 1980s the building trade started to slacken off and he found himself semi-retired. So he moved into property development and did very well. We've had our differences, my father and I, but only because we're both pig-headed and independent. We both stand up for what we believe in.

I had a stable and secure family background. There was just me and my younger sister, Leanne. We weren't spoilt, but we were fortunate in having everything that we needed, both materially and emotionally. I spent a lot of time with Mum's father, working for him in the school holidays; we were great mates.

Before St Andrew's I went to Opawa Primary School, which was one of the local area primary schools in St Martins, where we lived. For the first few years at St Andrew's I was one of the top academic students in my class but then, as I became more involved in sport, drama and playing in a band, my school marks slid down to average. I was, I suppose, a typical boy.

Dad is a great rugby man, but cricket was my main

sport. I played for the first eleven at school and was in a few representative cricket teams for Canterbury in various age groups until I left school. Cricket ran in our mother's side of the family. Singing ran in the family too, but I never could sing. In the seventh form I was the chairman of the committee that organised the school dance. I liked organising things and I liked being the leader. I had an opinion on everything and would say so, right or wrong. I think I've changed somewhat since then.

In the middle of my last school year I went to the air force recruiting officer in Christchurch and did the initial application tests and interview. Having got through that, I went to Auckland in the August school holidays for another selection process. Three weeks later I was told I'd been selected for pilot training, to start at the end of the year. Although I knew that the real test was still ahead of me, I was thrilled.

So in December 1986, three days after the school year ended, I joined the air force. It was the biggest shock of my life. Although, in some ways, it was like an extension of school – I had been wearing a uniform for most of my life so that didn't change – the discipline was firmer, and I had to fend for myself much more than I was used to in the way of washing, ironing and so forth.

When we started the training at Wigram Command Training School there were twenty-two of us. By the time we'd finished our flying training at Ohakea there were only ten of us left. On graduation we became pilot officers.

The training environment was artificial, in the sense that we belonged to a limited and rather protected little circle. Not until we had graduated did we discover what the air force was really about and how much it had to offer us. After graduation I was posted back to Wigram to do basic helicopter training, and then to Auckland where we flew the big Iroquois. I spent about eighteen months as a junior co-pilot on Auckland's Three Squadron before returning to Wigram. For the next year I did search and rescue, and tasks for the army and police. After another period in Auckland, I came back to Christchurch, flying as a captain, for more search and rescue work.

I found it a great way of life. We did so much for so many people, and every day there was something different. We were bringing people out of the mountains, hunting criminals, transporting wildlife to reserves, flying VIPs around. One of my highlights was flying Charles Upham, VC. Another was the five weeks I spent in Antarctica, dumbfounded by the incredible beauty of the place.

In the air force, everyone's career follows much the same pattern. You work hard and play hard, then work hard again the next day, and all the men you're working with are like you. They're motivated, they want to achieve things and they're fun to be with.

I first thought about going to Bosnia in 1992. You usually spent five or six years with the squadron, and by then I had done almost five years and was well down on the list for the flying instructor's course that I was keen to do. We were being inundated with pilots, so I would not be staying in the squadron for too much longer; I was facing the prospect of a ground job somewhere in Wellington or a job behind a desk in Christchurch for the next couple of years. I could not feel enthusiastic about such a future. But in 1992 my commanding officer considered I wasn't well placed to go to Bosnia.

I waited until April the following year. I was still in the squadron and we were about to leave for Hawaii to do some simulator training, when I heard I'd got into the Peace Force. I was over the moon. The United Nations was something we'd all grown up with – an organisation you could believe in.

We would leave for Bosnia in about four months. I'd planned to take a holiday at the end of our Hawaiian course and travel to other parts of the States, but instead I came back home to begin my week of peacekeeper training in Auckland at Land Force Command. It was there that I first met Kevin Dudley and Julian Tangaere, the two army officers with whom I was to travel to Bosnia. I also encountered Lieutenant-Colonel Paul Southwell, who would be in the mission area with us.

We spent the week on an intelligence-type briefing that included basic language training, medical training, communication, mine awareness and background to the war. We had psychological interviews, and we talked about trauma. We hired a rental car and did high-speed evasive driver training on the parade ground at Papakura. In hindsight, it was good preparation for what lay ahead of us.

The course took place three months before we departed, and those intervening weeks were a busy time for me at work. I was deployed to Fiji for an exercise with Iroquois helicopters for a couple of weeks, and I had a lot of gear to get together: flak jackets, helmets, sleeping bags, civilian clothing, first aid packs, winter clothing. The UN had organised all our travel, and the hiccups in the arrangements would turn out to be a gentle introduction to the bureaucratic nightmare that is the UN system.

Kevin, Julian and I finally left Auckland on 18 August 1993. All three of us got very drunk on that flight, which took us to London, then to Zurich, and on to Zagreb.

At each stop we had to hump our packs – a hundred to a hundred and twenty kilograms of gear apiece – so when we finally arrived in Zagreb, some two days after we'd set off, we were very tired. But we were excited, too. This city was the capital of Croatia: we were in the mission area and didn't quite know what to expect. But Zagreb, as we soon found out, was untouched. It could have been any city. Life was continuing fairly normally, apart from all the white cars with UN signs on their sides. We were met at the airport by one of the military observer training officers, a Norwegian. He had booked us into the most expensive hotel in Zagreb, US$70 to $80 a night for a room, while his own countrymen had been found a perfectly good hotel which cost only $30 a night. We didn't stay in our hotel for long.

The UN operation headquarters in Zagreb was a former barracks, and a bit of a rabbit warren. When we went there to sign on, we were faced with an incredible amount of paperwork. We were getting ID numbers and filling out the standard forms required when you are in a new military system, but then we had to take the pieces of paper around all the different units in the headquarters and have them signed by different people, to acknowledge that we were in the mission area. Then they gave us an advance on our mission subsistence allowance, and we started our military observer (MO) training.

So there we were, a collection of new UNMOs, sitting in a classroom at the UN headquarters, receiving our initial briefing from the chief military observer. I remember vividly how he sat up at the front of the room and cautioned us about becoming involved with local girls, 'especially the interpreters'. Anyone found engaging in that sort of relationship with locals would be sent home immediately. Even then, that directive did not impress me.

Once again, this training programme was about mine awareness, language training and first aid. But this time we also learned a little about the different sectors in our mission zone, and what was going on within them, and were told about the rules and regulations to which we, as observers, were supposed to adhere.

The United Nations Military Observers force later increased in numbers, but, when I arrived in 1993, there were nearly five hundred observers spread throughout the area that had been Yugoslavia. We were required to be unarmed, independent and responsible for our own food and accommodation (for which we received a *per diem* payment over and above our salary). Basically, the job involved cruising around the mission area to obtain information – 'intelligence' – and writing and sending reports. We usually travelled with two or three observers plus an interpreter to one car.

From the beginning it was apparent that we were a mixed group. There was a South American called Manero who couldn't speak a word of English. He had turned up with one set of military uniform, lots of civilian clothes, no sleeping bag, no flak jacket, and no helmet. He had something he called a 'medical kit', which comprised about five little bottles with a couple of pills in each. When he compared it with ours, his eyes popped and he was suddenly interested in bartering to bolster his equipment. It was obvious, even by that stage, that we would be working with untrained or incompetent people. There were some who clearly didn't want to be there, but had been dispatched by their countries regardless.

The training took five days, and in the evenings we – the Kiwi contingent – would eat down town at the local restaurants, accustoming ourselves a little to the ways of Yugoslav culture – their language, their food and their warm beer.

When the training ended we were posted; there was a posting available for one officer to Sector Sarajevo, one to Sector North and one to Sector South. There had been so much in the media about Sarajevo, which seemed to be the hub of the conflict, that I was keen to go there.

Setting aside the matter of historical conflict, the situation in Bosnia at that time was, in essence, that the Serbs were intent on incorporating Serbia, Montenegro and part of Bosnia into their vision of 'Greater Serbia', but there, in the eastern part of Bosnia they had mapped out as theirs, were these three pockets of land – Srebrenica, Zepa and Goražde – full of Muslims. If you're determined to exert your ethnicity and set up a 'great Serbian state', you don't want outsiders fragmenting the geographic sweep of your territory. When those outsiders have, historically, been your enemies, their presence is even harder to tolerate.

So the Bosnian Serbs had taken control of these Muslim enclaves, positioning their troops around them and setting up checkpoints to police all traffic entering or leaving those areas. Since each of those Muslim-occupied areas consisted of large valleys surrounded by mountains they could, in this way, be effectively controlled by quite small numbers of troops.

Kevin and I, both desperate to go to Sector Sarajevo, tossed a coin, and I won. So Kevin was going north and Julian south. We had a big night together before the three of us left Zagreb to go our separate ways.

I had been booked to fly to Sarajevo on one of the big Russian Ilyushin aircraft. Inside it seemed at first much like being on a Hercules back home, but the fold-down seats were extremely hard – it was all very basic and antiquated.

Virtually all the air transport in the UN mission area was organised by a Canadian company, which contracted aircraft and pilots from around the world to do the mission flying, and these big Ilyushins came with Russian pilots. (Some time later, my friend Marcus Kinzel took the same flight from Zagreb to Sarajevo and went up the front to check out the flight deck. He claimed that he found all the flight crew asleep, and that they were very displeased at being woken.)

Flying into Sarajevo was an experience in itself. It was common for arriving aircraft to take a round or two of machine-gun fire, and although – at least as far as I was aware – we weren't fired on this time, I wore my flak jacket and helmet from the beginning of our descent. Even when looking down from eight or nine thousand feet, you became aware of the extent of the damage and destruction in and around the city. As we flew lower, I could see whole streets full of houses that had been totally destroyed. Whatever I'd been expecting, this wasn't it. This was something I was used to in movies; I couldn't believe that this destruction was real.

At the airport there it was: the sandbags, the sound of gunfire in the distance, cars speeding across the tarmac, people in flak jackets and helmets. It was a hot summer's day and I knew I had to carry my gear to the UNMO headquarters in Sarajevo. Luckily I got a ride with some UNMOs in an armoured vehicle back to the PTT (sort of the equivalent of Post and Telegraph) building, part of which was being used as the Sarajevo UN headquarters. I remember that journey, looking out at half-demolished houses, their windows gone, at petrol stations burnt out – everything crushed or collapsed as a result of intense shelling and fighting.

The Egyptian driver said, 'Everywhere there are mines. This a very dangerous place to drive.' There were tanks, either burnt out or exploded, left half on the road and half in the ditch alongside. Other kinds of heavy military machinery and armoured personnel carriers (APCS), sat there like road barriers that had to be negotiated. I was still staring out incredulously at the destruction when we turned a corner into Sniper Alley.

This was a long, long stretch of road running from one end of Sarajevo right to the other. A very wide road, the kind we have in a town like Invercargill, but with massive high-rise buildings on each side. These huge apartment blocks had been hit by shells and you could see the steel innards with concrete still hanging from them. The tramway, too, had been hit and the tram was just sitting on the tracks with weeds growing up around it. If it hadn't been for the people travelling in cars (and there weren't many of them), it could have been a ghost town. Those initial impressions of Sarajevo will always be with me.

The PTT building was several storeys high and the UNMO headquarters, which occupied a small part of it, constituted the staging area for the mainly French, Ukrainian and Egyptian battalions based in Sarajevo. There were another premises closer to the centre of town, but this building was the hub. As well as being the UNMO sector headquarters, it was the head office for the UN humanitarian aid organisation, UNHCR (United Nations High Commission for Refugees), and housed all the different engineering units and support staff.

Here I learned from the senior military observer for Sarajevo that I was going to be sent to Zepa, which lay between the two other Muslim enclaves, Srebrenica and Goražde. Since the beginning of the war Muslim refugees from other parts of Bosnia had been flooding into those three pockets, to survive as best they could.

Going to Zepa with me was a Norwegian chap

called Lasse Farsund. We could leave at once, we were informed, but there was the matter of waiting for a clearance to come through from the Bosnian Serbs and this could take three or four days. Although I had a theoretical understanding of the situation regarding the enclaves, this was a severe shock to me. Why should we have to wait for a clearance? Who was running the show? Why did the Bosnian Serbs have so much control over UN personnel?

That first night in Sarajevo, Lasse and I slept in a transit room high up in the PTT building. This room, which we called 'UNMO Palace', had a big glass frontage and overlooked Sniper Alley. There were high-rise buildings directly across the road and we could hear shooting – heavy machine-gun fire down the street and, further away, shelling.

While we were waiting for Bosnian Serb approval we were to be working with a couple of UN teams stationed at Lukavica, which was in Serb-occupied territory just outside Sarajevo's city limits. We were picked up next morning by the Lukavica team and taken to their barracks. The UN mission there consisted of two teams: the Papa team and the Lima team. Each team consisted of about fifty observers, broken down into smaller groups of five or six.

The barracks functioned more or less as an ammunition dump for the Serbs. It had an area where the troops could sleep and there were a few tank pieces around – there was probably also some artillery there somewhere. While at Lukavica I was to meet three people who would figure significantly in the undreamt-of events that lay ahead of me.

The most important of these three was the Russian Sergey who, as senior UN observer on the Lima team, had the title of Lima Niner. I met Sergey on my first day at Lukavica, and even from that brief meeting it was clear to me that he had a lot of clout with the Serbs. Lukavica served as a command post for some of the Serbs' highest-ranking officers and the two other men who were to prove important to me occupied an office opposite the UNMO barracks. As liaison officers, they both spoke fluent English and worked as go-betweens for the local Serb commanders and the UN organisation. One I knew as Major Kušić; the other was a colonel called Goran.

Lasse and I were to stay in a local home being used by one of the UNMO teams. It was a common practice for the UNMOs to stay in local houses, paying the occupants rent for office space and a sleeping area. This one was a pleasant, well-furnished place.

It took us newcomers a while to understand what was going on. This was mainly because nothing was happening. We'd thought that this team would be out doing patrols, counting shells – how many were fired out of the city, how many were fired into the city – *doing things*. They reckoned they were resting and doing rotations at Mount Igman where they had an observation post. There was a tent set up and they were rotating shifts on a sort of forty-eight-hour basis. Apart from that, they drove to the PTT and back, delivering mail and buying supplies for the canteen there.

To my naive ears, the latter sounded like a jaunt, but then I went on the drive a couple of times, and it was frightening. We had to travel through the back of the airport – we actually drove across the end of the runway, or at least down the taxiway – and through into town. I was in my flak jacket, with my helmet on, and the men who were driving were obviously scared. They drove as fast as the cars would go because that particular part of the airport was subject to intense sniper fire. It was a piece of terrain where the Muslim and Serb soldiers could more or less see each other, and was also a favourite place for both factions to pick off UN cars and soldiers. No one seemed to have any compunction about shooting UN personnel; they did so regularly. So we kept moving. I wore my sunglasses and had my window open so that if a bullet came it would go straight through the vehicle rather than shattering the glass.

The airport itself was fairly well sandbagged and there were usually a lot of APCs around – not to mention plenty of French soldiers for the snipers to shoot at instead of you. They were the prime targets there.

Apart from those hair-raising drives, we spent a very boring and frustrating week in our house, waiting, writing letters, talking. I was relieved to get a couple of nights as a duty operations officer at the barracks. This involved manning the radios and taking down shooting reports – the grid references, where they came from, where they landed and so on.

By the time we left Lukavica I knew a little more about Sergey Turganov. This was a man who was well known and well liked by the locals; a man who was often drunk and who smoked like a train; a man who travelled at night and was scared of nothing.

Finally Lasse and I had our clearance to travel. We were advised that a man by the name of Sven would drive us through to Zepa, and we would be followed by a maintenance truck dispatched to do some work on the UN vehicles in the enclave. This trip was my first real look at the Bosnian countryside. It was only about a hundred kilometres from Lukavica to Zepa but, because of the checkpoints, it took us several hours. The road wound up through hills and from there you could look down on the city. As we drove we were passing the front lines of all the Serb soldiers in their bunkers, with a view of Sarajevo below.

Winding our way into the country, we came to our first checkpoint, which proved to be a mind-boggling experience. We had a clearance form, a faxed message which included our ID numbers. The checkpoint guards knew we were coming, and had their own lists, yet they still made us pull out all our ID cards and then checked the numbers. They examined our baggage and looked through the trucks to make sure that we weren't carrying anything unauthorised.

And that was just the first of a number of Bosnian Serb checkpoints where the procedure was repeated. The worst of these was at a place called Rogatica, which was run by a local man, a kind of self-appointed warlord who seemed to be a law unto himself. If he liked people, he would let them through; if he didn't, they would be stuck. Some UNMO teams, we were told, had spent nights there. (Although some of the observers, I was later to discover, didn't help their cause by sitting in their cars with the windows wound up, not even trying to converse.)

We got through that checkpoint, and through the last of the Serb checkpoints. All around us was beautiful country – forests and mountain ranges that reminded me of New Zealand. We drove through a number of old Olympic ski villages. I was still wearing my flak jacket and helmet; I didn't need to, but I didn't know where I was or who might be hiding in the trees. We'd left the main roads behind and were heading into the backblocks, winding and bumping over narrow, rocky roads, when suddenly, on the edge of the forest, we came to a Ukrainian checkpoint. And the man there wouldn't let us through.

I couldn't believe it. Here he was, a UN soldier, and

he was wasting time radioing down to his company headquarters in Zepa to get a clearance. 'For God's sake,' I thought, 'we're on the same side! We've got UN ID cards and we're wearing UN uniforms!' I wanted to throttle him, but he was, after all, following standard operating procedure. I didn't know it then, but this was just a small taste of what was ahead of us in terms of the UN bureaucratic machine.

We waited at that Ukrainian checkpoint for about forty-five minutes. There were a couple of crosses in the ground nearby, marking the deaths, I was told, of two Ukrainian soldiers. One, a local commander, had been involved in the black market and was killed by a Claymore – an anti-personnel mine activated from a distance by a hand-held detonator. The other grave, so the story went, was that of a drunk soldier who had been playing Russian roulette by seeing how many times he could run around the checkpoint without standing on a land mine.

When we finally passed through that checkpoint, we drove down a very rocky, windy and narrow mountain road towards Zepa. In some places it was barely one lane wide. There was forest, then there were high cliffs and sheer drops. We worked our way down the cliff face and eventually reached a small town at the bottom of the valley. There was a big river, the Drina, and small creeks, and great high mountains towering above. There were also some rolling hills, but even those were split by some very steep ravines. It felt so far out in the middle of nowhere that it was hard to believe anyone really lived there.

Driving into the town it was possible to form a good idea of how the people lived. You could see that they were farmers; they had orchards and crops and were working out in the fields, ploughing and planting. It was obvious that some of them were refugees; down by one of the creeks we had passed people who were living under a bit of canvas and a box that would have carried aid from a plane drop. The women stood in the river scrubbing clothes by hand and the children were running around barefooted, their faces dirty. You could sense the desperation.

As we drove into the town the rocky surface of the road became paving, maybe a hundred and fifty metres of it. This street was lined with very basic buildings – straight walls and none more than a couple of storeys high. The windows had no glass. Some had plastic, some had nothing. Everywhere you saw the signs of shelling and shooting. In the town centre we came upon a gathering of people, many of whom seemed to be just milling around, smoking, talking, staring at us as we drove past. They had nothing else to do. At a communal washing well, a group of women stood scrubbing clothes by hand while their kids frolicked in the water.

At an intersection we turned right and saw other UN vehicles and then the UN flag flying from a building which, I was to learn, had been a restaurant before the war. And the damaged buildings that were now used as houses had once been the commercial centre of a thriving little town – clothing shops, dairies, coffee bars... We pulled up outside the UN headquarters in Zepa, and saw, by the plastic-covered windows that it, too, had been damaged.

The three or four members of the UN team who were on hand took Lasse and me for a quick tour of the premises. In the main room was the restaurant's big serving counter and, in another large room, a collection of beds had been laid out. There was also an office, with a couple of computers sitting on a table, and a radio set up.

I was looking around me, wide-eyed and eager. 'This

is it! I'm in the middle of a bloody war zone, and this is where I'm going to be living for the next three or four months. Yes,' I thought, like a typical Kiwi, 'this is all right. *So let's just get on with it.*'

chapter six

Zepa

A New Zealander called Howard Duffy had led the first UNMO team into Zepa in May 1993, only three months before Lasse and I arrived there. The enclave encompassed eighty square kilometres of mountains and valleys. Fifteen to sixteen thousand people, a large number of them refugees, lived in the town of Zepa and the many villages within the enclave's perimeters.

Conditions at UN headquarters were fairly basic. We were lucky to have a generator that occasionally provided us with hot water, but there was no permanent shower set-up and, when Lasse and I arrived, there was little in the way of food.

The French team leader was moved on within our first few days, to be replaced by a Dutchman called William Joziasse – Jos, as we called him. In his midfifties, he was an experienced soldier (he'd been in the Green Berets) and a very nice man. In a team you quickly form opinions about those you'll be working with and it was clear that, in this case, there were the competent ones and the rest. Two of the former were Marcus Kinzel, a Swiss architect who was doing a year's tour of duty as a territorial soldier, and Bert-Jan (BJ) Harte, a Dutchman who was stationed in Germany as a regular tour soldier and was on a six-month mission. BJ and I became very close friends. Many nationalities, the Dutch among them, were doing six months, but we Kiwis were there for a year.

The worst of the incompetent ones was a very lazy chap from Ghana. Everything was just too hard for him; he would lie on his bunk, day in and day out, counting down the days he had left in the mission area – eighty days to go, and then seventy-nine. He was an extremely difficult man. I had to bite my tongue many times when dealing with him.

The daily routine for our team began at seven a.m. with a bit of breakfast or coffee, then a team meeting to sort out what we would be doing that day. Our main duty was patrolling and there were three basic patrol routes: one went to the south, another – a long patrol that took up most of the day – went north, and the third patrol travelled the middle area.

On the southern patrol you had to stop at various Ukrainian checkpoints. As the initial peacekeeping force in Zepa, the Ukrainians had set up and operated eight checkpoints positioned around the edge of the pocket in a sort of front-line area. Their soldiers, who lived at the checkpoints, had the job of recording any breaks in the ceasefire, so when there was any shelling they counted the rounds and listened for the explosions. We would collect these details from them and incorporate them into a daily situation report (sitrep) that we sent, at the end of each day, to Zagreb.

On each of our patrols there would be two UNMOS

and an interpreter. The three interpreters attached to the Zepa UNMO team were Denisa, Boriša and Miroslav. There was a shortage of Muslim interpreters and both Boriša and Miroslav were Serbs who had been given jobs in Sarajevo by the UN, but then had to work in Zepa. Although their sympathies didn't lie with the Serb side, being a Serb in a Muslim enclave that was under siege from the Serbs was hardly comfortable.

The patrols were always interesting. As an established UN safe area, the enclave was supposed to be free of warfare, but in fact there were always little skirmishes going on around the outskirts. Under the terms of the UN agreement when it was made a safe area, the local people had to surrender all their weapons. Of course they didn't do so entirely, and the Bosnian Serbs used this as a reason for making life difficult for both the observers and the people of Zepa.

Despite the indignation it aroused in the Bosnian Serbs, the fighting force within Zepa was very small. The population consisted mainly of elderly people and children, with perhaps fifty to a hundred poorly equipped soldiers among them. And they weren't professional trained soldiers, just men and boys who had done a year's compulsory military service. But until the UN moved into Zepa and raised its flag, the place was being shelled regularly, so the minor attacks that followed the UN arrival were a vast improvement. The people in the villages soon grew to appreciate the UN presence, and the UN humanitarian aid convoys that followed. Most of the locals treated the UNMOs with respect, and were always wanting to stop us and give us fruit off their trees and *rakija*. As with any home brew, everyone's *rakija* was the best! It has a very high alcohol content, and although it is extremely hard to drink, we often became drunk on the stuff.

The roads we travelled on those patrols were rough and rocky. We bumped and shuddered around and, by the end of the day, felt absolutely exhausted. We were using four-wheel drive Toyota Landcruisers but the vibrations and the juddering made it seem like being back in the Iroquois. The driving was exceptionally difficult and we soon sorted the good drivers among us from the bad. There was a story about a Jordanian UNMO whose vehicle started slipping backwards on a mountain track. He just let go of everything and started talking to Allah. The co-driver had to reach over and grab the handbrake to stop them from sliding off the cliff. You didn't allow some team members to drive very much if you could help it.

On our patrols we called at the Ukrainian checkpoints to ask what had happened in the last twenty-four hours. And they would reply, 'Oh, there was a burst of heavy machine-gun fire at five past five last night, followed by three single shots of small arms fire and then we heard a grenade explosion.' We would also stop and talk to the locals through our interpreter, and they would tell us a little bit more. Then, at the end of the day, we would write our report and send it to the UN, or to our headquarters in Sarajevo to be processed and forwarded to Zagreb. We would say, 'There is some small arms activity around the pocket ...'

After a few weeks of this, I began to think, 'So what?' They weren't going to do anything about the information we sent, so all this effort seemed pointless. But an UNMO's life was to patrol and to report, and that's what we did. And every night we would sit down at the tables, have a meal and get gratefully drunk.

You would see things on a television screen and think that you knew what to expect, but those were just moving pictures. When you were there, living among those people and getting to know them, the emotional impact was tremendous. There they were with no electricity, no really nutritious food, inadequate clothing, missing teeth; some were living under cardboard boxes or trees. And by the time we arrived they were used to it, which only made the situation worse. Perhaps I let it affect me too much, but some of us just couldn't help becoming emotionally involved.

Because the Bosnian Serbs would have their tanks rumbling round on the outskirts of the enclave, the people were living in constant fear that their lives were about to be destroyed. Some were hysterical with terror. Old women would cling to us and weep. It was deliberate psychological warfare – to keep the Muslims in a state of fear and deprivation, to wear them down into submission. It was more effective than simply killing off the Muslim soldiers. Naturally, therefore, anything that might ease the people's burdens met with resistance or obstruction from the Bosnian Serb authorities.

For instance, they didn't want the food aid convoys coming in. They would search them at every checkpoint, and if they found anything that wasn't approved they would remove it – I remember once that there were great delays over the removal of an 'unauthorised' spade and shovel. Sometimes they would let the trucks through to within fifteen kilometres of Zepa – so the people would know they were almost there and would be waiting – and then, on one pretext or another, turn them back.

To be fair, the Bosnian Serbs weren't the only ones to jeopardise the aid supplies. The convoys consisted of twelve large trucks, and the drivers and aid supplies came from various parts of Europe. Some of the Russian drivers would stop the trucks and start selling shoes off the back, just before they got into Zepa.

If we as observers wanted to make things happen,

we were required to go through UN channels. We did that. Day in, day out we punched out messages to Geneva, and to the Red Cross, saying that these people desperately needed aid. We asked, too, for helicopters to evacuate people who were dying. But nothing would happen, and this made us feel utterly helpless.

To a degree, I could understand. Here was a huge organisation, employing around thirty thousand UNPROFOR personnel, including five hundred military observers, so there were bound to be organisational hassles. But the fundamental problem was that the civilian side of the UN and the military side didn't connect. On the one hand, you had people working office hours with lunch breaks and free weekends; on the other, you had shocked UNMOs trying to deal with crises as they arose. If we asked for approval of a project or course of action it would be an urgent necessity, but if it was going to cost money we needed permission from the finance branch and that could take two or three weeks.

We'd have meetings with the local Serb commander. We'd say, 'Look, we want to put an end to the shooting. We want the oppression to stop. We want you to let all the convoys through.' But there was always this or that reason why none of these things could happen.

The Ukrainians didn't help much. They had the resources to assist the people but most of their energy seemed to go into maintaining their own checkpoints. They sold food and fuel on the black market when it could have been used to assist the locals. They would argue that their own families at home were at least as badly off as the people of Zepa, but the black marketeering was consistent with their general attitude. There was no sense that they and we were there for the same purpose. They wouldn't even make their truck available to transport food from the drop zone down into the village. They were supposed to provide us with fuel, and they did, but would never let us in to collect it. We'd have to wait for ages in the compound. You had the impression that they were deliberately baiting us. It made me very angry.

We had a weekly meeting with the Ukrainian commander but, when it came to the behaviour of his troops, he seemed to turn a blind eye. The attitude of the Ukrainians seemed to be sympathetic to that of the Serbs, and we felt that, in most respects, they were on the same side.

Impartiality was an important issue. As UNMOs we needed to have the trust of the Muslims, the Bosnian Serbs and the Croats, so we couldn't be seen to be helping one side or another. But such a rule does not, of course, allow for human nature. You're thrust into the middle of a situation where people are dying of cold or hunger, so what do you do? Is it partial of me to build a house so a family has shelter? Is it partial to give someone some salt or a couple of kilograms of flour, or a teat so a baby can drink milk?

My decision was that such help was simply humanitarian and that partiality would involve divulging military secrets or transporting weapons or war equipment. I would also carry and post letters people wrote in the hope of tracking down their missing relations; all the observers carried such letters. I also brought in clothes, cigarettes and mail, although we weren't supposed to. I did this for people from each of the ethnic groups; that seemed as impartial as you could get, so I had no qualms about my actions.

The senior national observer from New Zealand, who was working in Kiseljak, had announced that he was going to hang anyone he caught smuggling such things through checkpoints, so if I'd been caught I could have been severely punished, or at least repatriated in disgrace. But at the same time there were lots of things, including some large sums of money, that I refused to carry in for people. But it was so difficult. People were constantly clamouring at you. Can you bring me back some razor blades, some tobacco, a pair of jeans for my child? At first you wanted to do something for everyone, but sometimes you grew tired of being asked.

Despite the frustrations of the job, we put in long hours. In theory we worked for thirty days straight, then had six days off. Such a period of leave gave those from the Netherlands, the Czech and Slovac Republics, Russia or the Ukraine time to travel back home to their families – provided, that is, that the airport at Sarajevo was open and the flights were running.

I didn't take compensatory time off (CTO) for the first forty-five days. We were short of staff and, since I couldn't get home to New Zealand and would only be going somewhere else in Europe, it seemed more important that the other men saw their wives and children when their leave was due.

For many of the men, life revolved around CTO. Because they were always waiting for their next break, they were not productive in the mission area. They simply didn't want to be there. Some had children my age and for them this posting was a sideways career step and generally unwelcome. Some might have been keen originally but, after the first few months, they had begun to ask, 'What the hell am I actually doing here?' So they settled for collecting their pay cheques and anticipating their next leave.

These men seemed to have shut out what we were seeing every day. They didn't let it affect them. I couldn't do that; right from the first moment, I was bombarded emotionally. I felt ashamed to be among these people because I was so well off compared with them. I had decent clothes and I knew where my next meal was coming from, whereas they had nothing. They were embarrassed about their circumstances and I was embarrassed about mine. To come from a very fortunate and affluent country and suddenly find yourself in the middle of such poverty and fear made you feel both humble and thankful.

You were seeing, too, how war reduced people to the basics of humanity, to mere survival instincts. One man killed another for thirty kilograms of flour. He had fled into the safe area with his wife and young child and they had nowhere to live, no money, nothing but the clothes they stood in. So he killed, for thirty kilograms of flour. That shocked me. I kept thinking about it. In that same situation, what would I do?

We wanted to help everyone but we couldn't. We could, however, do small things such as giving them plastic sheeting to cover broken windows or holes in their buildings, or sparing them some sugar or salt or fuel. We even found accommodation for some refugees. We would approach people and say, 'Look, we know you've got a spare basement. Will you please let this family live there?' But there were sixteen thousand people, so we had to assess the worst cases. But even the minor assistance we could give clearly meant a great deal to the people concerned.

We'd been on the mission a couple of weeks, and my sense of frustration was just setting in, when Lasse Farsund suggested a way of helping the refugees. On our patrols we'd been visiting two refugee camps, Cavčići and Purtići. The inhabitants had been driven out of their homes in villages outside the area enclave and had come to Zepa because it had been designated a safe area. They had collected together in these two camps, and they had nothing. They were living under bushes and cardboard boxes, on the side of a hill. They had no clothes. They had no money. They had very little food. They were trying to make the best out of a bad situation, but winter was only a couple of months away.

The town administration didn't seem to be doing much for these people. One of the men who worked on the local council was thoroughly corrupt. He sold a lot of the convoy aid and pocketed the proceeds. Mattresses and other items that were supposed to go to the refugee camps never reached them and this caused a lot of bad feeling.

So here was something practical we could do: we would build houses for eleven or twelve families.

We were told that we could take trees from the forest, and we managed to borrow a chainsaw. Then we sent the refugees into the hills to find the trees and cut them down. We bartered with local men who owned trucks, giving them fuel in return for transporting the timber. We found a man who knew how to build suitable houses, and we had him working for the refugees in return for a certain amount of fuel. (Fuel was a very precious commodity. You couldn't get it from anywhere other than the UN supply, and the locals could trade it at incredible prices if someone had the money to pay. Fuel was survival. It meant you could run your chainsaw to cut down trees, to burn more wood, to heat your water, to cook your food if you had any.) And we smuggled nails and plastic through the checkpoints between Sarajevo and Zepa.

Almost every day we would call in to see how the refugees were progressing, to encourage them, to arrange for more wood, more nails, more plastic... Little by little we managed to get those houses built before the winter settled in. Simple houses – four walls, semi-detached, with roofs made out of parachute fabric that had come down with the air drops, and plastic sheeting. When they were finished, the people were absolutely delighted. They named their village after us, UNMO, and, incredibly, they even put on a big celebratory feast for us. They somehow acquired a sheep, which they roasted on a spit to give us a wonderful meal.

Unfortunately, that day there was trouble in Zepa. During the feasting, I was racing around like a madman dealing with the effects of some shooting. I had driven up to Ukrainian checkpoint seven with Boriša, the interpreter, and while we were there we heard machine-gun fire, some of it directed at us. So we rushed back to town, about a twenty-minute drive, grabbed our flak jackets and helmets and returned to the checkpoint. We spent some time with the Ukrainian warrant officer, who was behind binoculars in a sort of dugout, trying to position whoever was shooting at us. A few rounds went over our heads and there was an air of tension, but nothing more developed.

Most likely the reason for the shooting was a celebration that was to take place the next day in Zepa. An important Muslim commander by the name of Naser was coming down from Srebrenica with some hundred and sixty of his men, and that was causing tension among the Serbs. They might, therefore, have decided to take some action. Quite probably, Naser and his men would have walked through Serb lines, killing a few Serbs on the way and causing damage and destruction. That would certainly have raised the level of hostility a notch or two. In fact, earlier that day I had been up at the refugee area and there was a burst of heavy machine-gun fire, so loud that I dived behind the car. The locals took no notice and laughed at me for taking shelter. Heavy machine-gun fire is loud at the best of times, but in those valleys the sound reverberated and was particularly frightening if you weren't used to it.

The UNMOS had been invited to the Naser-centred Muslim celebrations being held at the top end of the mission area; a couple of carloads of us went up, with our interpreters. It was like a carnival day, with a game of soccer and a big feast afterwards. They had music playing through a speaker rigged up to a car battery, and there was a lot of drinking going on among the two thousand or so people attending.

Naser and his men were there, although we couldn't identify them. At one point the interpreter, Miroslav, and I were standing beside a group of men. A fierce-looking Muslim, standing on the other side of Miroslav, said something to him in Serbo-Croat. When I asked what he had said, Miroslav, looking most uneasy, replied, 'I think we should leave.'

'Why? What's the problem?'

'He said he's going to kill me.'

Miroslav was badly scared. His was a well-known and traditional Serb name, even though he didn't consider himself a Serb and his sympathies lay with the Muslims. We'd been at the celebrations a couple of hours by then, watching the match, wandering around, but that was it – BJ and I jumped into the car with Miroslav and rushed him back to Zepa.

Back at the HQ we had a talk about it. Jos was away at the time and BJ was acting team leader. Boriša, it turned out, was also scared because he'd been receiving evil looks from some of Naser's soldiers who were in town. We weren't going to risk our interpreters, so we got permission from the Ukrainian lieutenant-colonel for Miroslav and Boriša to spend the night at the Ukrainian headquarters. These were only about a hundred metres up the road, in an old schoolhouse, but they were more or less barricaded and had barbed wire around the perimeter, because they had fuel and food and all sorts of desirable things inside.

Who knows if these precautions were necessary? Certainly a few of the Muslim soldiers were seen hanging around our UNMO headquarters later that day and in the evening.

We were quite often made aware that some of the people in the enclave didn't want us there. They saw us as ineffective, doing nothing more than getting in the way of their fighting. You'd hear UNMOs saying that we should just get out and let them get the war over with. Thousands of people would be killed but sometimes we felt that we were simply delaying the inevitable. Better, maybe, if it were over and done with.

We knew from the media that the UN was at an impasse; the international response to the war was fractured by power games between Russia and NATO and the hidden agendas of the various nations. Russia had close ties with the Serbs; Germany was in all probability selling and supplying weapons to their old allies, the Croats; the Americans' Vietnam experience had made them wary of interfering in civil wars ... and so it went on.

About once every two weeks we would drive to Sarajevo, to buy food and fuel, to pick up our mail (for which we were always desperate) and perhaps to attend special briefings or to take out one of the team who was going on leave. Each time you made this trip you needed a clearance, which had to be applied for seventy-two hours in advance. This angered me; I felt that we were trapped in the enclave, at the mercy of political whim.

We'd apply for clearance on the capsat, an excellent piece of equipment that resembled a kind of fax machine and which sent messages via the satellite. We would write the message on the computer, punch in the destination and out it would go, to bounce off the satellite and hook up with the computer to which it was addressed. Apparently it was very expensive to run, but it gave us total flexibility in the mission area. We could put it in the back seat of our car, drive off somewhere and sit on the top of a hill and watch a battle take place, then type out progress reports, punch them in and send them off to Zagreb or Geneva or wherever.

Our clearance requests were sent through to the UNMO office in Pale, where the Bosnian Serb parliament and headquarters were. A liaison officer would then pass the requests on to the Bosnian Serb authorities, who would decide whether they would allow us to travel through the Serb part of Bosnia. We would be hoping that the clearance would come through at least a day before we travelled. Sometimes it didn't and we weren't able to leave. We could only speculate as to the reason. Possibly they were moving men, or artillery, that they didn't want us to see. In effect, the Bosnian Serbs had total control over us.

Providing we'd surmounted that first hurdle and our clearance had been confirmed, we would set out. Every time it was like my initial trip to Zepa, only in reverse. We would pass through the Ukrainian checkpoint, just on the outskirts of the enclave that was our mission area, and reach the first Serb checkpoint. There they would either make us wait or, if they were in a good mood, let us straight through. They blamed the delays on their need to check that our clearance had been authorised. That might have been true, but sometimes they'd make us wait there for up to two hours and it certainly felt as though they'd just decided to frustrate us.

Further on there would be another couple of checkpoints that were not usually a problem, but then we'd reach Rogatica, run by the obstructive man that we'd encountered on our first trip to Zepa. At Rogatica anything could happen: we might be turned back, we might be made to wait all day or all night, or we might be subjected to full body searches. Depending on which soldiers were on duty at the time, we might have the films taken from our cameras, or the cameras themselves might be confiscated. They might remove our cigarettes or fruit. The object was to harass us, to a greater or lesser degree, depending on whether things had been going well for them at a military level.

Certainly, at Rogatica they had some reason to be tough on UNMOs. The checkpoint was on the route you took from Gorazde, the southernmost enclave, to Sarajevo, and UNMOs from Gorazde had been caught smuggling things in for the locals. The latter liked to barter – you couldn't buy anything much with cash, but cigarettes, in particular, were in big demand; they loved smoking. So the UNMOs there survived on a barter system, exchanging cigarettes for beef or whatever. The Serbs had a fairly good idea of what was going on and so would hassle them. The last straw, for the checkpoint soldiers, was when some UNMOs returning to Gorazde were caught taking in a number of Muslim prayer books and a huge amount of money – thousands of deutschmarks. They had the books in the back of the car! The UNMOs in Gorazde became so desperate that they resorted to removing the door panels from their cars and hiding cigarettes inside the linings. But the Serbs somehow found out about this, and began taking the panels off to look inside. They would even open the bonnets of the vehicles and do thorough engine searches. The UN authorities became rather upset about this.

The other interesting story concerning the UN team in Gorazde was that their local interpreter, a woman, was running a well-organised prostitution racket. A British friend of mine who had visited there said the interpreter arrived on his doorstep to offer him a woman in exchange for two cigarettes. (This was not as cheap as it sounds – for one cigarette people would pay up to US$2, which went quite a long way in local currency.)

Once past Rogatica, we would wind our way through the hills and the countryside until we were among the Serb front lines and trenches. The soldiers would always wave us down, wanting some fuel or just to talk. From there we would drive down towards the city and the inevitable mad dash across the exposed airport tarmac, with our sunglasses on and the windows wound down. Beyond that there were the French checkpoints, then a stretch of Bosnian Serb territory followed by the Bosnian Muslim checkpoints before you entered Sarajevo. Then all that was left was the drive down Sniper Alley and you were at UN headquarters in the PTT building.

The hundred-kilometre journey could take a very long time, and we very seldom made a return trip on the same day. Almost always we would stay the night in Sarajevo and organise fuel and food for the team. We'd spend the evening in the international bar. Because there were so many Frenchmen in the PTT building, they had their own French bars, but there was also an international bar where the rest of the UNMOs, and the interpreters, drank. A lot of the locals worked there. It was just a small room that they had kitted out as a bar, but we would get drunk there.

Getting drunk was a real release. I couldn't sleep in Sarajevo if I was sober. With all the heavy machine-gun fire and shelling going on, you could not get a decent night's sleep unless you were unconscious. In all, I spent about fourteen nights in Sarajevo and I got drunk on every one of them. Besides, we had good times in the bar, getting to know the locals, learning the language, just talking. Boriša and Miroslav would come with us on these trips to interpret for us at the checkpoints, and they knew all the locals.

On our very first night in Sarajevo, Lasse and I had met a young woman called Sanela, who worked at that time at the restaurant in the PTT building. When we met up again she had got a job as an operator at the telephone exchange. We became good friends and she was a big help to me in my efforts at learning the local language.

One of the purposes of our trip would be to get food and fuel for the team; we'd get through ten to fifteen twenty-litre jerry cans of fuel before our next journey. We would buy our food supplies from the French kitchen at the headquarters. There was a chap there who would take us out the back to the freezers and the food area and, under his guidance, we would help ourselves. He would charge us for this food, and the money would go straight into his back pocket. We didn't sign anything, or see any paperwork, and he would be looking over his shoulder when the money was changing hands. The men who ran the French kitchen had a very nice bar, fully stocked with spirits, and they had video recorders, a TV and fridges.

There were clearly some illegal deals going on. They were cheating us, too, given what we received and what we were charged. So whenever our supplier had his back turned, I would grab a couple of extra chickens or a slab of steak, and put it into the van. I believe the UN officials eventually discovered how the place was operating and the system was made a little more accountable. Not all the food we got would make it back to our team headquarters. On the return journey the checkpoint soldiers would all want to look at our fresh supplies and invariably we would end up giving them some to ensure that they'd let us through with the rest.

Once, when we were loading up our trailer at the French kitchen, mortar fire came flying in and landed about a hundred metres away from the compound. I'm not sure whether it was a shell. I didn't hear it until it had almost hit the ground and when it did it shook the place from top to bottom. I went into a pre-natal crouch, pulling my flak jacket up as high as I could around my ears. You never grew accustomed to such things, or to the knowledge that it could happen at any time. Kiwi UNMOs Jim Finlayson and Mike Morgan, who had served in Sarajevo and Gorazde during the heavy fighting, could tell some real horror stories about the close calls they'd had. It amazed me that no New Zealand UNMOs were killed. A couple were injured by mines and mortar shells. I was lucky, although I had a couple of near misses while I was in Zepa.

One happened on the way back from my first week off. I had gone to Hungary for my leave break (which was by then much needed – I'd discovered it was necessary to get out of the place every so often in order to keep myself sane) and was travelling back with another UNMO. We called him Rudi (his real name was Ismael Khairuddin) and he was a major in the Malaysian army. Rudi and I had taken a train to Zagreb, and then flown to Sarajevo in a Russian plane.

The PTT building was only an eight-minute drive from Sarajevo airport, so we thumbed a ride in a minivan driven by a Danish man. Rudi and I climbed into the back and two Egyptian officers took the seats in front of us. We'd travelled a couple of minutes out from the airport and were driving through a heavily war-damaged area with the odd crack of gunfire, when suddenly there was a metallic bang as our vehicle was hit. This happened quite often, so we drove on, and then one of the Egyptian men started to whimper. My first thought was that he was scared, but then we looked over and saw that there was blood everywhere. Oh my God, he'd been hit! As the chap went into shock, Rudi and I tried to get out a bandage and do something for him. The other Egyptian was a shivering mess, in shock himself. For some reason, those two weren't wearing their flak jackets or helmets. Rudi and I were, and so was the driver.

The bullet had come in at an angle and gone through part of the Egyptian's arm and his hand, which had been up on the seat in front of him. Luckily it had missed the bone. It had embedded itself in the seatbelt behind the driver's head, just an inch or so from his ear. This meant it must have gone right past me. 'It could have been me,' I kept thinking, 'it could have been me!'

The other close call was my own fault. Lasse and I and a relief interpreter called Nikola had set off for Sarajevo, and on the way Nikola wanted to call in on a friend of his, a rather pretty young woman who produced a bottle of *rakija*. Lasse, especially, was a man who liked to drink, so after making a few toasts one bottle led to another. Having finished two bottles of *rakija* in a very short time, we were completely drunk. But off we went, Lasse driving, Nikola in the front passenger seat and me in the back, drifting in and out of consciousness.

At one stage I came to and saw, in the car beside me, a Serb soldier with a gun. Carrying soldiers was absolutely forbidden; carrying an *armed* soldier was unthinkable. Another time I regained consciousness to find that we had a girl hitchhiker travelling with us. Remarkably, we had no problems at all at the checkpoints. The soldiers seemed pleased to see that we were fallible beings who could have a good time.

'What's the story,' they would ask, 'with that guy in the back?'

'Oh, he's unconscious. He's smashed out of his mind.'

And they would laugh and let us through.

By the time we reached Sarajevo I was awake, though far from sober. Lasse was ready to go on leave and, as we headed in through the airport, there was a Norwegian Hercules on the tarmac, with the engines running and the back still down. These planes flew in and out of Sarajevo delivering humanitarian aid, and Lasse used to fly in them; he'd had a job dealing with the freight down the back of the aircraft, so he knew all the men involved. Suddenly we were driving right up to the ramp and Lasse was jumping out of the car into the back of the plane! Then they closed the door and he was gone.

It was incredible. There we were, Nikola and I, left on the tarmac, drunk, with the French military police heading our way. I leapt into the driver's seat and started pulling away but, next moment, a French officer was standing in front of the vehicle, muttering something in French or incomprehensible pidgin English. (The French made very little effort to learn English. Since they had more troops in Sarajevo than any other country, they thought, rather arrogantly, that everyone should be speaking French.) I just shook my head and drove away as fast as I could, in case they decided to pursue us.

My plan was to drive across to Kiseljak, which is about thirty minutes north-west of Sarajevo. A Battle of Britain celebration was to be held there, and I knew that some of the other Kiwi UNMOs were planning to attend. I had been to Kiseljak once before so I knew how to get there, but I was still half drunk. It was a winding road and there were checkpoints on the way because you were crossing through Bosnian Muslim territory into Bosnian Serb territory and then into Bosnian Croat territory. Many of these checkpoints had tank traps or barricades in the form of big concrete, triangular blocks that sat on the road. These blocks, which had anti-tank mines in front of them, could be pulled out across the road to block it off in a hurry. And there would be trip wires that could be set off by someone standing some fifty metres away.

I rounded a corner to find one of these checkpoints ahead of me. A big APC coming in the opposite direction was manoeuvring through the barrier and I was pressing towards it, thinking that, when it came through, I'd sneak in quickly behind it. Then, suddenly, it stopped, or perhaps stalled. Glancing at my speedometer, I saw that I was going quite fast. I thought, 'My God, I'm going to have to stop', so I slammed on the brakes – and began to skid towards the anti-tank mines. They were designed to destroy tanks and I was driving a four-wheel-drive Landcruiser. Miraculously, we stopped, literally inches from disaster. The terror of the experience certainly sobered me up rapidly.

My stay in Kiseljak turned out to be worth the scare. It was good to get together with some Kiwis, especially the air force fellows, and talk not just the same language but the same jargon. After spending your time with people of so many different nationalities, it felt wonderful being with my own kind again. There were also a couple of parcels waiting for me, and there were newspapers, so we could catch up on what was happening back home. One of the boys had a video of an All Black test match and, of course, we all stayed up to watch it.

Looking back on my time in the Zepa mission I sometimes think I was too idealistic. Certainly I was naive initially; I trusted people and believed everything they told me. Then slowly I began to realise that this was a war, a dirty war in which survival was everyone's aim. We made the best of a bad situation. We tried to improve the lives of the people at least a little. That was all anybody could do.

Zepa village, with the tower of the mosque the only dominant feature.

Aza's family's summer house, high in the hills and very close to the Serb front line.

Before the war: Aza with some of her girlfriends in Zepa.

Aza with her brother Alija (kneeling, centre) and some of their cousins in Srebenica, one year before the war.

Aza's family (her mother is on the far right) and neighbours in her lounge/bedroom/living area.

*Jos with Aza's grandmother at Purtici, above,
and with Mustafa, Aza's father, below.*

Three brand-new Kiwi UNMOS on their arrival in Zagreb. From left to right, Kevin Dudley, Brent and Julian Tangaere.

Getting to know the locals. The UNMOS with a refugee in the forest.

Brent, Aza and her mother in front of their house in Purtici.

The Serb tank that Aza's brother Alija helped to destroy.

*Refugees' houses built by the UNMO officers.
The occupant of the rear house killed another man for 30 kilograms of flour.*

*Refugee boys tend to a lamb roasting on a spit, given as thanks for
the UNMO's gift of fuel.*

Aza's little sister Alida thoroughly approved of the developing relationship between Brent and Aza.

ABOVE: Complete with Kiwi jacket and epaulettes, Aza learns to drive in Brent's UN vehicle.

RIGHT: Aza and Alida, woken early one morning by the UNMO team.

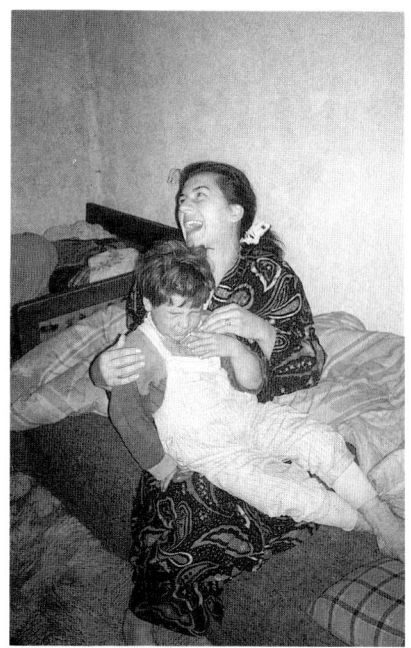

*One of Brent's few summer outings with Aza.
With them are Denisa the interpreter and Mahmud the Jordanian.*

*Aza grinds coffee in preparation for one of Brent's many coffee stops
when on patrol.*

Brent planned to propose to Aza just after this photograph was taken. Instead snipers' bullets sent them racing for their lives.

Sanela (left) and Indira, the two interpreters based in Sarajevo who translated Aza's letters for Brent and helped him to obtain her passport.

The first steps towards freedom. Aza poses with Boriša for a picture that would later be blown up to look like a passport photograph.

Free at last! 9 June 1994, the momentous day when Aza escaped from Zepa to Belgrade.

New clothes, a new life.
Aza and Branco at Marko and Marija's wedding in Belgrade.

The wedding at Ohakea, so many worlds away from Zepa.

Aza and Brent at Ohakea air base.

part three

Aza and Brent

chapter seven

Meeting

It was my first day in Zepa. Marcus Kinzel, the Swiss man from the UNMO team, had offered to show Lasse and me around and introduce us to some of the locals. That part of the township consisted of just one street and we – Marcus, Lasse, Boriša and I – were standing talking to someone when I saw this beautiful woman.

From the moment I saw her I could not take my eyes off her. I had seen pretty women in Bosnia, but often when they smiled some of their teeth would be black or missing. But this was a truly beautiful woman, wearing stylish clothes; you could tell she had class by the way she walked and held her head. She looked so out of place among all that destruction and deprivation. There was a man on her arm, whom I assumed was her husband or boyfriend.

Marcus called out to her and she came over to talk to us. Introducing myself in very basic Bosnian, I struggled to find the words for some small talk. As she and Boriša chatted away, even without understanding a word, I could tell that she was a happy, good-natured person.

She was with us for only a couple of minutes and then she was gone again. I'd forgotten her name in the first five seconds – in a foreign country people's names are coming at you constantly and you don't take them in.

As we walked off I asked Boriša, 'What was that girl's name again?'

'Aza.' Boriša looked at me. 'Don't worry, we'll get to visit her on patrol. You'll be seeing her every now and again. We'll call in to her house for coffee.'

'Oh,' I thought, 'okay.' Then it went out of my head until that night after dinner.

'That girl, what was her name again?'

I had to ask him once more. Aza. I couldn't get her face out of my mind.

I had walked into Zepa that morning to try to get some pills to ease my grandmother's rheumatic pains. It was a nice day, fine but not too hot, and I was wearing a skirt, a cotton-knit top I had borrowed from my girlfriend and comfortable shoes for walking. On the way into town I was daydreaming about what I might have been doing at that moment if the war had never happened. Daydreaming is a Pisces characteristic; Pisceans have a private dream life.

When I reached Zepa I met up with some friends – Amir, who was the husband of Denisa who worked for UNPROFOR, his brother Samir and their cousin. Amir said Denisa would be back from patrol soon and we should all go to their place for coffee, so I said I'd meet them after I'd been to the medical centre. But the doctor had gone off somewhere, so I returned to tell Amir that I would come for coffee later. Samir, who was the boyfriend of a friend, said he'd wait and come with me. He and I were standing talking when three UNPROFOR men came along with Boriša. One of them was the Swiss, Kinzel, who had called at our place a few times with Denisa. He and Boriša saw me and came over to say hello. We were introduced to the other two. One was a Norwegian in normal military uniform; blond hair, blond eyebrows, blond eyelashes and blue eyes – nothing there to interest me. But the other man was from New Zealand and he said, in my language, 'Nice to meet you.' Right away I thought, 'Ah ha!', and gave him my biggest smile.

His hair was very short and he was wearing sunglasses and a light brown uniform with the sleeves rolled up. His boots were made of some kind of fabric. Those would never see him through the autumn, I thought, but didn't say so. He reminded me a bit of an American Marine – rolled-up sleeves, big muscles, small brain. And, though he had stripes, he was young, like the Marines who came to Zepa without any understanding of what they were letting themselves in for, looking for an adventure.

It was two or three days later, when we were on patrol, that we called on Aza. Everyone, it seemed, knew her and all the UNMOs seemed to be enthralled by her. Parking next to a couple of buses that had been shot to pieces, we walked up a rocky driveway until we came to a gate. Beyond that there was a basement with a new tin roof on it. This was Aza's house. Beside it there was a pile of wood and a few fruit trees. Aza came out and invited us inside. As I stopped at the door to take my boots off, I noticed the shoes and gumboots beside the doorstep. They looked like the shoes you see in rubbish dumps, all worn out, full of holes. We all went into a sort of dining room, which contained beds and mattresses and a cooker in one corner. There was washing hanging around the walls and you could see that this was where they slept and ate; they had a little room out the back where they stored food and clothes. This is what people in Zepa had been reduced to.

We sat down on cushions and Aza made us coffee, heating water on the stove and grinding the beans. This was my introduction to Bosnian coffee, which came black and sweet, in very small cups which they kept refilling. There was Aza, her grandmother, her little sister and her aunt. Everyone was sitting around smoking and talking and Boriša was busy interpreting. Aza's grandmother, a very nice woman, was sitting there taking everything in and, when BJ rolled a cigarette, she asked if she could have one. Many Bosnians loved to smoke and although these people were growing their own tobacco, they had no papers so they'd use old newspaper or anything they could find. So it was nice for them to have some European tobacco and proper cigarette papers. I had some cigarettes with me. I don't smoke but I carried cigarettes around and handed them out as gifts. At Aza's home my cigarettes were very well received.

They were running low on candles and I remembered I had a couple in my survival kit down in the car so I ran out, fetched them and gave them to Aza's grandmother. She was delighted. I also gave her a couple of batteries for her radio, and I'd found a can of Coca Cola in the car for Aza's little sister, Alida.

This wasn't special treatment; we would give such gifts to many families. They would invite us into their homes and offer us coffee and immense hospitality and this was our way of returning the kindness.

The next time he came he was with Denisa, and he'd learned a little more of our language, but that time they didn't stay long. The third time he found us all – me, my grandmother, my sister, my brother and sister-in-law and some neighbours – around a cauldron pressing sour apples (to drink the juice, and to make wine). By then, part of me was looking forward to seeing him but I was telling myself that I didn't like him at all.

This time it was Brent and Boriša who came, so I stopped work and we sat around the table. Brent's watch was showing the wrong time; when I pointed this out he said it was still on New Zealand time, but he didn't change it. Whenever I looked at the face of his watch, which was hours out, I started to giggle. Finally he said, 'If I move it to the right time, will you promise to stop laughing?'

'Yes, okay.'

So he reset his watch. I had been smoking and now, through Boriša, I asked Brent if I could please have another cigarette. Brent said something and Boriša began to laugh.

'What did he say?'

'He said, "Why don't you just ask for the whole packet?"'

I was furious. 'You idiot,' I thought. 'Do you think I'm hanging around because of your smokes?'

'Keep your cigarettes then,' I snapped.

'I was joking,' Brent protested.

'Well, I'm not, and I don't want your bloody cigarettes.'

Boriša was laughing even more now, and Brent was trying to push the whole packet on to me. 'Take them.'

'No, I don't want them. I really don't want them.'

Perhaps I was being over-sensitive. They both began insisting that I take the packet of cigarettes, so eventually I did. Again Brent said something and Boriša told me, 'He says just because he's giving you these doesn't mean he likes you.'

I started to walk away. 'Tell him I don't like him either – the only thing I like about him is his shirt.'

Soon I was seeing her every two or three days, depending on my patrols. The middle patrol went near Aza's house but I might be on one of the others or be rostered as duty officer. It was a matter of luck.

I was visiting her home regularly but I still could speak only a few Bosnian words and she couldn't speak English. All our small talk was done through whichever interpreter was there that day. Our communication was entirely dependent on these people, and it could make a great difference which one we had, because they all had rather different agendas.

Miroslav was the best, because he was happy for us to get to know one another and enjoyed interpreting. Boriša, on the other hand, had his own designs on Aza and, although he was a good interpreter, he wasn't wanting to make things easier for me. Then there was Denisa, who liked to gossip away to Aza, and wasn't too interested in interpreting for me.

With or without conversing, I was becoming more and more attracted to Aza. I didn't need words to know that she was a woman of strong character with a kind heart. She had endured so much already, yet she was always smiling – she had a wonderful smile.

We were never able to spend any time alone. Apart from interpreters and other UNMOs, her grandmother was always there, or her brother, or her mother and father, whom I met later. And dear little Alida, then about five years old, was always at Aza's side; those two were inseparable. At that stage I didn't mind all the company. I wasn't intent on falling in love with her – what was the point? I would be there for only three months, maybe, and if Aza had any interest in leaving Zepa she would have done so before the war started.

At first we were just friends. Then, after I'd met him a few more times, I told myself that, although we were still just friends, he was a closer friend than all my other companions. Soon I was thinking about him a great deal. Will he call at our house today? The patrol route didn't quite come past our place but it did pass the water well that was about five minutes' walk away. So I began to go down there every morning, and wash my clothes slowly.

When I ran out of dirty clothes, I began washing things that were perfectly clean. At other times, I would take water containers and go to fetch fresh water. I'd tell my grandmother I was off to fetch water so we could have a nice drink.

'But we have plenty of water,' she'd say.

'I'll go, anyway.'

It was good being there with my grandmother because she thought I could do no wrong. My parents were staying at the summer house but they would sometimes arrive and stay for a couple of days, and that would put an end to my trips to the well – especially if we had any visitors, because then my father expected me to make coffee and talk to them, and empty the ashtray. If I wasn't there my father would ask where I'd gone, and my mother could hardly say, 'She's gone to fetch water for the fifth time this morning.'

I could spend the whole morning at the well waiting for the UN vehicle to come past. If Brent was in it he would stop to say hello, and agree to come back for coffee after they'd done the patrol. Then I would quickly finish my washing and go back home.

One day, after we'd met a few times, he drove by and stopped and I saw that his eyes were red. I was worried for him. 'What's happened?'

'It's nothing,' he said. 'Just a cold or something.'

Later, Denisa's husband, Amir, told me that Brent had spent a night on the town in Sarajevo. He was drunk, and he was with a woman. I thought, 'So maybe he's got a girlfriend. Shall I ask him?' No, I couldn't.

Another day, maybe a couple of weeks after we first met, he came after work in civilian clothes – jeans and a white shirt – and he looked so beautiful. He came with Miroslav who wanted his hair cut, and he sat outside with my grandmother while I was inside cutting Miroslav's hair. Brent was teasing Miroslav about the haircut, and Miroslav said, 'Don't ask me what he's saying, you don't want to know!' He liked Brent. He said he was a very nice man, who saw our situation as a living hell. I said I could understand that.

Through Miroslav, Brent then said to me, 'If you come to New Zealand, I'll get you a job as a hairdresser.'

I said, 'Yes, that would be fine.'

Then Brent said something and Miroslav told me, 'He says, no, it wouldn't be fine. You should have a better job than that.'

'Thank you,' I said. 'But I would be quite happy cutting hair.'

'No,' he said. 'You deserve more. I wouldn't let you be a hairdresser.'

That was the first really nice thing that anyone had said to me for so long. I knew then that he was seeing in me someone who was of value.

Soon after that Brent arrived with Denisa and a Jordanian soldier called Mahmud, who wanted a haircut. Denisa said Brent wanted to go on the mountain to take some photos and would I come too and cut Mahmud's hair up there? I asked my grandmother for permission, but she was worried because my parents were due.

'What would I tell them? You'll get me into trouble.'

'I think it's tomorrow they're coming. It's definitely not today.'

'Well, good luck,' she said. 'But if they come, it's your funeral.'

So we all drove up through the little villages and on to the mountain, but all the time I was worrying that we'd meet my parents on their way down. When we turned off the road I asked to have a little drive. They were all shouting, 'Oh my God, Aza, stop. You're going to kill us.' But it was all right; we were just on grass. It was a beautiful day and we sat down and I cut Mahmud's hair. Then I asked Brent if he wanted a haircut and he said, no. I thought he didn't trust me to do a good job.

He had some chocolate bars. He gave one each to the others then said, 'Oh dear, there are no more left.' Teasing me. Then he gave me one, and another one for Alida. 'I'll ask her if she got it.'

'Of course I'll give it to her,' I said. I knew that, as she always did, Alida would insist I had half.

Brent then gave me two sheets of paper with English phrases translated into Bosnian: 'How are you?', for example, and, for a restaurant, 'What can I have to eat?' I was really pleased with that.

On the way back we stopped to examine some unexploded grenades lying in the bushes, and walked down to get a closer look at a handsome horse. Brent took photos; he had an excellent camera. I was aware of him all the time, but we kept a distance between us. And, for me, there was the nagging worry that my parents would be home, but they weren't.

The day before I was due to go on leave, Boriša and I were drinking coffee and *rakija* at the home of a man called Enver, a wealthy man who'd owned a big trucking business before the war. His house in Zepa had been his holiday retreat, but he'd been trapped there when war came. He was ethnically a Muslim but his circumstances differed hugely from everyone else's. He had plenty of food, two cars, petrol, cash, and anything he didn't have he seemed able to acquire. He gave the UNMOs a lot of items, including the use of his chainsaw for the refugee houses.

When Enver left the room Boriša began to confide in me how much he liked Aza. He said he hoped I would help him to spend more time with her. I muttered, 'Yes, Boriša, of course.' But I had no intention of helping him in that way. He was a nice, peaceful sort of man, Boriša. Even though he was a Serb he avoided the army, and even resisted visiting his family in Sarajevo in case he was grabbed and conscripted. Before the war he'd worked for a TV station, and he spoke good English. I felt sorry for him because he was extremely keen on Aza and he must have been aware already that there was something between us.

After forty-five days I went on leave and met the Malaysian major, Rudi. I was heading for Budapest, but first spent a couple of days with Rudi in Zagreb, trying to get a visa for Hungary. When Rudi and I went shopping, I bought Aza a watch, some make-up and a pair of boots; I also found some gumboots for her grandmother and a doll for Alida. In my hotel I sat down and tried to write a letter to Aza, then threw it away and wrote another, then threw that away. I was trying to say that I was falling in love with her and I wished she could come to New Zealand with me, but I knew it was impossible.

It was on our way back from Sarajevo airport that the Egyptian soldier in the seat in front of me was shot.

That jolted me into realising how short life could be, and what was important and what wasn't. At that point a kind of resolve, a sense, at least, of possibility, was forming in my head.

I smuggled my purchases from Zagreb back into Zepa in my bag. The first chance I had to see Aza, after returning from my leave, was at the end-of-year breakup party in the schoolhouse. I took her back to my room afterwards and gave her the presents, but she was worried and embarrassed about being there and about what people might say. She wouldn't take the gifts with her in case she was seen.

So I mooted the idea that we should have a dinner at her place one night and I would provide the food. I made sure that I was on the next trip to Sarajevo, and when we went to the French kitchen I took a couple of extra chickens and some extra vegetables, which I left with Aza the following morning. We invited Denisa and her husband Amir and I told Jos that we'd been asked to dinner – even though I had invited myself. Boriša and Miroslav were upset about not being invited. I told them that I couldn't take everyone. The last thing I needed was Boriša's presence.

I took along the gifts, and my little stereo because they had only a radio, and we had a most enjoyable evening. Aza had created a feast: roast chicken, vegetables and salad and a bottle of red wine. I hardly ate anything, although Aza was trying to force the food on me. I wanted it to be for them – a rare chance to eat well. Of course there was candlelight – there was no choice. I had taken along a photographic book on New Zealand and, as we looked through the pages, Aza marvelled at the beauty of the country, with Denisa interpreting. Aza sat very close to me, with her leg touching mine, as she leant over the book, asking questions about my work back home and flirting with me. It felt good.

That night I knew for certain that I was besotted. I had never felt anything like this before in my life. I would do anything to be near her, to be able to talk to her. Although I still put in long hours doing my job, from that night onwards my life revolved around spending time with Aza.

We also began to exchange letters, which gave us the privacy our meetings never had, and it was only through what she wrote that I learned that she felt as I did. I had given Aza an English pocket dictionary, and on my trips to Sarajevo I'd asked my friend Sanela to teach me some endearments so that I could write those in her own language – loving phrases such as *Volim te dusa moja*, 'I love you, my soul', and *Volim te budala mala*, 'I love you, small fool'.

One day, not long after this dinner, I'd driven up Aza's driveway to call in for a few minutes and, as I was backing out, I looked up at Aza, who was standing on a big high boulder near the stream. She said to me, in English, 'Goodbye, my love.'

This took me completely by surprise, because she'd hardly spoken any English to me, and her tone was so sweet and sincere. I was so happy that I lost concentration, drove too close to the bank and caught the car on a huge rock. It took ten minutes of rocking by some locals to free me.

I didn't want to fall in love with Brent because it seemed such a hopeless situation. From the night of the dinner I knew that I had feelings for him but I pushed them down. I didn't want other people to guess how I felt and make a joke out of it, and I didn't want to get hurt. Whenever I was with him I watched how friendly and thoughtful he was to other people. I could see that he was a good person, that he had something special that set him apart from all the other men I knew. Denisa and Amir were always telling me how nice he was, how kind. I liked to hear that but when Denisa started saying how much Brent liked me, I would try to appear indifferent.

Alida was the only one who really knew how I felt; I never kept anything from her. She always seemed so much older than her years – I could talk to her just as if she were my own age – and she knew how to keep a secret. She could tell when I had problems. My little sister was like an extension of me, we could tell what each other was thinking and when she wasn't with me it was as if a part of me were missing. We liked the same things and the same people.

The first day that Brent came to our place she would sit and watch him, then run off to play, but in a couple of minutes she'd be back again, watching. I think she knew how I felt about him even before I did. She would make plans for me. In the morning when I was washing her face she would say things like, 'I was thinking last night about your problem, and I think we should…' That would make me laugh.

When Boriša said anything negative about Brent, even as a joke, Alida would be furious and berate him. One day after this had happened, Boriša produced two big chocolate bars as he was leaving and said to her, 'These are for you.'

She said, 'I don't want your chocolate.'

'But I got it especially for you. I want us to be friends.'

'No,' she said, 'I don't want it.' But we could all see her mouth watering.

'It's Brent's chocolate,' Boriša said. 'He told me to give it to you.'

Alida beamed and took the chocolate. 'Thank you,' she told Boriša. 'But don't think this makes me your friend.'

The night of the dinner, when Brent gave Alida the doll, she was so overcome with happiness and embarrassment that she cried.

I was so worried, that night, that my parents were going to arrive; at the slightest sound outside I would run to look, although no one knew why except my grandmother. If my parents had come, it just wouldn't have been the same. I sat very close to Brent that night, but not so close that he'd think I was trying to climb on to his knee! I knew that soon Brent was going on leave, and I knew I wanted to see him some more.

Not long after that night I became ill. I had no energy and no appetite – I thought I must have caught a cold from spending all those mornings with my hands in water! When I went into Zepa to see the doctor, I dressed up because I always liked to look my best. Many women had started to think, 'Why bother? I'm stuck in this place, what's the point?' But I'd always tried to look good, and since Brent arrived I'd been trying even harder.

The doctor examined me. 'What's happened to you, Aza?'

I told him it was just a cold, but I could see that he was worried about me. He said I must have a penicillin injection every morning for the next few days, and must also return for a drip infusion.

When I was put on a drip by a doctor at the medical centre, Brent, Denisa and Amir came to visit me. Brent was looking at me with such concern that I told him he could sit on my bed. The doctor, who was a friend, and the two male nurses muttered that they weren't allowed to do this, so why should he be? When I ignored them, they said, 'That bloody Kiwi, he comes here and steals her. What does she see in him? What's so special?' I told them to be quiet.

Brent said he would drive me home. I'd been hoping he would but I wasn't going to ask. By now I was a hundred per cent certain that I loved him, but I still wasn't sure if he felt the same about me. When he dropped me off at my place, he said he would come and pick me up next day and take me for my injection.

I'd started out walking before he came. In the car I let my hand slip down just beside his on the gear lever. I was in such a turmoil. When I touched his hand, for a moment he did nothing, and I was rigid with embarrassment. Then he put his hand on mine.

That first morning I'd arranged to take her for her injection Jos and a couple of others were leaving to go on CTO. I needed them to take off before I could jump in the other car and collect Aza, but they had a flat tyre. I was looking at my watch, impatient to be gone and there they were fiddling around. I was thinking of Aza having to walk – and she was really weak for those first few days; she could hardly stand up – and also about missing out on seeing her.

Time was ticking past, so I grabbed the spare from the back of the jeep, got out the jack and leapt into the job like a dinkum Kiwi. Those wheels are heavy but I had one off, another on and the nuts done up in record time. 'Right, I've done it for you. Now, just get out of here. Go.' Then they discovered they were almost out of petrol.

By the time I got up the hill Aza had been already walking down for about ten minutes. I screeched to a halt beside her. On the way down, seeing her hand sitting beside mine, I threw caution to the winds and took it. We had been talking, but suddenly there was a tense silence. For me that was it. I was in love!

Generally the UNMOs would stay in any one mission area for only three or four months and then be moved on, although some stayed for six months. When Jos returned from his leave, he put in a request that my stay in Zepa should be extended. By then I was deputy team leader and Jos had only another couple of months to go; he felt that if I stayed and took over as leader it would provide continuity. He argued in his request that we had built up an excellent rapport with the locals and that I was doing a good job. He did everything in his power to keep me in Zepa. Jos knew I was in love with Aza and, although at first he'd warned me against becoming involved, when he saw that it was too late, he did all he could to help us.

By now there was open competition between me and Boriša, although I was already the winner. Miroslav used to liken it to a game of golf, with me putting on the eighteenth hole while Boriša was still getting his clubs out of the back of the car. We thought this was funny, but for Boriša it was no joke. If he was with me and we'd stopped at the well to talk to Aza, she would stand on my side of the vehicle, touching my arm as she talked. Boriša would become very angry.

Alida, Aza's little sister, didn't like Boriša and never hesitated to tell him so. The poor chap would receive nothing but criticism from her, whereas she adored me – I could do nothing wrong in Alida's eyes. I would feel sorry for Boriša at times, but I was certainly not going to step aside for him.

Whenever we'd landed the short patrol, which got us back early, and Aza had come into town, Boriša would tail us. I'd say to Aza, 'Let's go to Denisa's place', and Boriša would invite himself along as well. And by then I knew he wasn't always interpreting correctly for me. So, if I returned from patrol before Boriša, and Aza was in town, Amira and I would race to get us all to Amira's house so that Boriša wouldn't know what was going on.

One night when Brent was away on leave, Boriša walked the five kilometres to our house to see me. It was a risky thing for him to do on his own because everyone knew he was a Serb. He came for coffee. Even then, I still thought he was just a very friendly boy. Later, when he sent me a love letter, I was surprised and angry. I wrote back to say that as far as I was concerned we could either be friends or nothing at all. A couple of weeks later he apologised, saying that he understood and that we should be friends.

After the course of injections had finished, I let my family think that I still had to visit the doctor, so that I would have a reason for going into Zepa. Friends there would try to give Brent and me a chance to be alone. I remember calling in one day when Brent was duty officer. He was working on the computer and I was sitting on the sofa. Amir had gone to make coffee or tea, closing the door behind him, and then Jos came in, his head turned. 'I can't see a thing, I'm not looking.' Both would knock hard before they came in.

But, that time, nothing happened. We just sat there, looking at each other like two puppies.

The next time we were at Denisa's place, she called Amir out to the kitchen to help her make coffee. 'I must go help my love,' Amir was smirking. 'You two just relax.'

He left us sitting there side by side on the sofa. I was so nervous. My stomach started to rumble – I hadn't had any breakfast – and I tried to drown it out with talk.

Finally we kissed and Brent told me that he was in love with me. I hardly heard him; my mind was lost.

When Denisa and Amir came in with the coffee Amir's eyes went straight to my face, and I could feel it burning. 'Oh, Aza,' he said, 'something's happened to your lipstick.' He was wearing a big grin.

It was then that I registered that Brent had said he was in love with me. I hadn't said anything. There was nothing I could say. I knew then that, from almost the first time I saw him, I had been waiting for him to say this. But I was also afraid. We love each other – so what happens now? Whatever we do, it is going to mean trouble for him and trouble for me.

As we all left the house, I took Brent's hand. I was so happy at that moment. The person I loved also loved me. So often it doesn't seem to work out that way. I was scared for our future, but that couldn't prevent the happiness. I didn't want to wait for Brent to get a car to drive me home, but insisted on walking. But I wasn't really walking, for all the way my feet didn't touch the ground.

Right from the start Amir was on our side, smoothing the way. He could speak a little English and he and I were good friends, so one day I asked him how to say, 'Will you marry me?' and 'Will you come with me to New Zealand?' in Bosnian. He wrote the words down for me.

Then, after patrol on a day when Aza had come into town, I told Jos I wanted to take a car and drive Aza down to the river to take some photos. He agreed, but warned me to be careful. We weren't supposed to transport the locals; if you did it for one person, everyone would be wanting a ride somewhere.

So Aza walked up the road and around the corner,

where I picked her up and took her down to a spot by the Drina. And I was thinking, 'I'm going to do it! I'll ask her to marry me.' Then I'd tell myself that this was crazy; I'd leave and we might never see each other again. I didn't even know if I'd be staying in Zepa for the next three months.

On the way we stopped off to look at the mass graves of the people who were butchered in Višegrad and floated down the river. There were all these little crosses in the grass. Sometimes I felt that the horror and ugliness around us increased the truth and beauty of our relationship. We were trapped in this bubble that was our love for each other; nothing else really mattered to us.

Driving down a zig-zagging road to a peaceful and picturesque spot, we parked the car, walked down the grassy bank and sat by the river. I'd brought along some chocolate muesli bars that my mother had sent me. We were nibbling on those and talking in the limited kind of way we could manage with my Bosnian and her English. It was a lovely afternoon. I took some photos of her, still keying myself up, until finally I decided, 'This is the moment. Say it.'

As I opened my mouth to speak, a burst of machine-gun fire reverberated all around us. It was so loud and close that I expected a blast of hot lead. It was scary. We were right on the edge of the safety area; the mountains all around us were occupied by Bosnian Serbs. When the sound had stopped we decided that it was just a warning shot and we could stay a little longer. I was trying to pluck up the courage to try again when a second burst rang out, even closer, so we ran to the car.

As we were driving away up the winding, rocky road, Aza suddenly said, 'War is good.' I stared at her. We'd just been shot at. How could she be saying such a thing? Then she added, 'If it wasn't for the war I would never have met you.'

Outside Aza's house we kissed quickly, but she was looking around anxiously in case we were seen, so this wasn't the moment for me to try once again to propose.

A couple of days later we were sitting in Aza's house, with Alida and their grandmother, and we were using my dictionary to help us find the words to talk about everyday things. The sheet of paper on which Amir had written his Bosnian translation was in the dictionary and, on an impulse, I pulled it out and laid it in front of Aza.

'Will you come with me to New Zealand?'

'*Vrlo rado*,' she said – 'very willingly'.

When I saw the words, I blushed, but my grandmother noticed nothing; she was sitting on one of the beds and, as she always did, nagging me about Brent. 'Offer him something to eat. Ask him if he is hungry.'

I said, 'No, he's not.'

'How do you know? You haven't asked him.'

I always found this embarrassing. If I gave him something to eat he might not want it; if I asked him what he wanted we probably wouldn't have it.

While my grandmother was speaking I was looking at Brent and thinking, 'Oh my God.' Then I said, 'Yes.'

Alida came sneaking up to the table. 'What's going on here?'

'Nothing, nothing.'

It was 13 November, Alija and Fatima's first wedding anniversary, so later they turned up with my mother and father. Brent stayed for dinner and all the time we were looking at each other and smiling until it was Alija's turn to ask, 'What's going on with you two?'

'Oh nothing,' I said. 'We're just happy about your

anniversary.'

With my father back home, I knew I wouldn't be able to keep going to Zepa so, before Brent left, I told him I thought I should go to the mountain for a visit. I would take Alida, while my parents kept my grandmother company. I said I would see him at the water well and tell him when I was planning to leave. So I was back at the well, washing and washing, with my hands all red from the cold, and on the second day Brent came past. I told him we would be on the road by nine thirty the next morning and that he should just pick us up on the roadside.

Next morning we told our parents that we'd decided to walk to the mountain. It was foggy outside and my father thought it was too cold for Alida to walk all that way. Of course, Alida knew that the plan was for Brent to take us, and she was protesting: 'No, it's not. I want to go, please.' My father usually hated it when she whined, but this time he gave in and we left very quickly. Brent and Denisa caught us up and we jumped in the car. Brent seemed very quiet and I sensed that something was wrong. At the summer house only Fatima was home; my grandfather was away minding the sheep and Alija had gone to fetch water. Brent was going to take us to find my brother so that we could walk back with him. But now he said, 'I've got something to tell you.'

'What?' I knew it was bad.

'I'm leaving soon.'

Suddenly, all my happiness was shrinking away. I wanted to cry. He was waiting for me to say something but my throat had grown so tight that I couldn't speak. If I tried to say anything, I knew I would start crying. Running into the summer house and shutting myself in a bedroom, I wept, but quietly. Then I walked out again and said, 'Let's go and find my brother.'

When Alija asked if I was all right, I said I was, but really I was terribly sad. When Denisa said she needed to go home, Brent said he would take her home and then return. I thought, 'But he won't come back. Not now, not ever.'

The fax came through from Sarajevo that morning. Jos read it first and he took me aside. 'Kiwi, I've got some bad news. You're not staying, you're going.' Ironically, given how frustrated I often felt with our role in Zepa, this should have been good news. Many of the observers would have welcomed it. The worst part was that I was about to go on leave in Germany for seven days, with BJ and his wife. I'd be back for only three days before I had to fly out forever.

On my way home from the mountain, after I'd told Aza, a man waved me down wanting fuel for his chainsaw. He took us to see the house he was trying to build. When I gave him five litres of petrol, he produced some *rakija*, but I declined, saying that the fuel was a gift, not an exchange. But he kept insisting and Denisa said I must accept.

I took Denisa home and checked with Jos that it was all right for me to go back and have dinner with Aza. It was a long drive from our headquarters to the mountain; even by the shortcut it took about forty-five minutes. So as soon as we'd had our team meeting I jumped in the van and rushed off. I could feel the time we had left together ticking by and I wanted to see Aza as often as I could.

When I arrived, with my *rakija*, there was a drinking session in progress. One of the visitors was the Ukrainian commander from checkpoint six. I was so upset about leaving that getting drunk seemed a good idea. The Ukrainian was drinking heavily and urging me to match him, turning it into a competition between us, and the drunker I grew the more I noticed him trying to flirt with Aza. She could speak some Russian and I could see that he was trying to chat her up. I sat there, becoming increasingly jealous and upset, until finally I said, 'Better dead than Red.'

Alija burst out laughing, and the Ukrainian was asking what I had said. He was pestering Aza to tell him, so finally she translated it as, 'Better drunk than dead.' But the others laughed so he wasn't convinced. I said to Aza, 'Tell him.' So she did. Alija tried to smooth things over but the Ukrainian was outraged and decided to leave immediately, so Alija drove him back to his checkpoint.

By then it was around midnight and had been raining hard for two or three hours. When it was wet the shortcut track was a quagmire, impassable even for four-wheel-drive vehicles. Aza's grandfather tried to persuade me to stay until morning, but I was drunk and determined to get back to Zepa that night. Jumping in the wagon, I pressed off down a grassy slope on to the track. I drove a fair way down, surprised at how well I was doing, and then I became stuck. I realised I wasn't going to get any further, that I hadn't sobered up and that it was still raining. Somehow I managed to turn the car around and drive back almost to Aza's house. But as I was climbing up on to the grassy verge, I lost all traction and started to slide backwards. It was like being in an air trainer – that moment when you run out of air speed and you're just hanging there and then you tail-slide for a while. I slid backwards until I ended up in a hollow and, no matter what I tried, I could not get that wagon out of there. It was pitch dark and still teeming with rain. I got out and stumbled back up the hill to the house.

I could see that Aza had been crying. She gave the

car keys to Alija, who went back down and somehow got the car out, but by then I'd decided it was a good idea to stay. I slept the night in the same room as her grandfather and Aza got me up at five a.m. and made coffee. I had to be back by seven for our team meeting and I knew I could not take the forest track.

It had been a bad night for both of us, and I was going on leave the next day. Before I left, Aza gave me a letter to take with me. It was written in Bosnian, so when I got to Sarajevo I asked Sanela and Indira to translate it for me. Indira handed it back to me.

'I can't translate this for you, Kiwi.'

'Why not?'

'It's too sad. I'm sorry, I just can't do it.'

So Sanela translated it for me, and cried as she did so. The letter explained how, until she met me, Aza hadn't cared whether she lived or died, but now she had a reason for living. I kept all Aza's letters – they were what got me through the months that followed.

Ever since Aza had said that she would go to New Zealand with me I had been lying awake at night, racking my brains over how this could be done. She would never be granted permission to leave and I could not smuggle her out in a car, because travel requests were passed through the Bosnian Serb government in Pale and IDs were checked and rechecked during the journey. Our vehicles, and sometimes we ourselves, were searched. It just seemed hopeless.

The one useful thought I had was that, if I were ever to find a solution, I would need Aza's passport. I reasoned that even if I lost it or had it taken from me, or if nothing ever eventuated, her passport was no use to her anyway. She wasn't going anywhere and, besides, it had almost expired.

Next day I left Sarajevo on a direct flight to Frankfurt in an American Hercules, then took a civilian flight to Bremen, where BJ and his wife met me and took me to their place. Although BJ was a Dutchman, he was stationed in the north of Germany, near Hamburg. I spent a pleasant, relaxing week there trying not to dwell on the thought of leaving Zepa and Aza.

I also met up again with Pat, a Canadian I'd met and got along well with when I passed through Frankfurt on my previous leave. Pat, who was deputy senior military observer in the Krajina area, which was my new posting, told me several stories about Sergey, who was his boss. According to Pat, Sergey had been transferred from Sarajevo, where I had met him during my first days in Bosnia, because he was achieving more, and proving to be more effective, than the UN generals. Sergey had friends in high places; he was a man who could do anything. From our brief meeting, Sergey had made an impression on me. Now our paths were going to cross again. He seemed to offer a glimmer of hope for Aza and me, and I resolved to get close to the man.

I got back to Zepa on 25 November and was leaving on the 30th. Five days – and the first two of those were spent making a supplies trip to Sarajevo. With only two days to go, Boriša and I picked up Aza and her family and drove up the mountain to say goodbye to Aza's grandfather and Alija and Fatima. We spent a few hours there. Aza cooked us a delicious meal and her father, Mustafa, and Boriša and I talked and drank. When we dropped Aza and the others home, I told her I'd come and see her the following night, my last in Zepa.

I took Joseph, the Czech man in our team, with me that night. We arrived after dinner. Aza's grandmother and her parents were there, as well as Aza and Alida. Joseph could speak Bosnian, so it was good to have him there. While he was talking away to Mustafa, Aza and I could very quietly say all those painful and poignant words: 'I'll wait for you, don't forget me.'

I hardly heard what he was saying to me. My thoughts were churning around and around. 'Why does he have to go? Is there something I can do to keep him here? This is the last time I will ever be with him.'

The day before I had given him my passport, because he'd told me he might need it if a chance came for me to escape. My passport seemed like a piece of my life and it took a lot of trust for me to give it away, although I trusted Brent more than I'd ever trusted anyone. Now Alida began to cry. She came to me and said, 'He's not really going away.'

I remember Brent saying, 'How can I help? I'll give you one thousand American dollars.'

'No,' I said, 'no.' Money would buy us petrol to cut wood for the winter, and other things that the Ukrainians might have to sell, but I didn't want him to think that my feelings had anything to do with what he could give me. I didn't want him, one day, to look back and say, 'I had a girlfriend when I was over there. I was able to help her out with some cash.'

My mother was listening to this conversation and later she said, 'He offered you money?'

'Yes.'

'What for?'

'You know, to help us out.'

'And you didn't want it?'

'No.'

She smiled. 'That's most unusual for you.'

We were there for a couple of hours, thinking that this might be the last time we'd ever see each other and just putting off the inevitability of saying goodbye.

When I finally said I must go, Alida clutched my hand, saying, 'No, no, no,' and began crying. Then everyone was saying goodbye. Aza came outside to see us off; her father was there too. It was dark by then and icy cold. I kissed her on the cheek and the last thing I said to her, in Bosnian, was, 'I will come back for you.'

chapter eight

The Plan

That final night at Aza's we didn't even manage a dignified departure. Joseph and I jumped into the car – we were both rather drunk, and I was upset, so Joseph was driving – and started to back down the hill, when we hit a fallen tree. It jammed under our back wheels and we couldn't get free; our tyres were sliding on the ice. After a few attempts, I leapt out and tried to move the log. Joseph was swearing, and had to go back for something he'd left behind. All the commotion brought Aza's father down. He gave us a hand and we eventually freed the car and set off again.

Joseph was very understanding. He had a wife and three daughters at home. 'She is a very good woman. With a woman like that you would be very happy.' He was an excellent friend to me, Joseph. I was devastated to hear the following March that he'd died in a car crash.

When any of the UNMOs were leaving, the people they'd grown close to would come to say goodbye. So next morning, as I was packing my gear into the car, a group of people gathered. Among them were Denisa and Amir, and Fadila, our cook, and her family. There were also some of the little children to whom I used to give sweets. Everyone was half crying and saying good luck and shaking hands.

I felt that I was abandoning them. The UNMOs were their lifeline. Of course there were always new observers coming to replace those who left, but the locals didn't know who they would be or what they'd be like. These people would build up a relationship with someone on whom they could rely and then he'd be gone and they'd have to start all over again.

In every way, leaving Zepa was very hard. I'd thought about going up to say another goodbye to Aza, but once had been bad enough – I just couldn't go through that again. As we drove out that day, I felt that I was deserting her and her family. It seemed very likely that I'd never see her again. All the same, I was determined that, whatever it might take to keep us together, I would try.

In the car with me were Boriša, Joseph and a Jordanian chap I'd never liked. He could never accept the fact that I, only a flight lieutenant – the equivalent of captain—, had been made deputy team leader, while he was a major and therefore a rank higher.

I had Aza's passport stuffed down my underpants, and I was also carrying some letters for people. I knew the Rogatica checkpoint would be the difficult one and, sure enough, the soldier on duty began to sift through all my gear. He pulled out sleeping bags and shook them; he went through my music tapes and listened to a couple in case there were messages recorded on them; he started to shake my books to see what fell out and he came uncomfortably close to the letters I was hiding. If he'd found those, he would have done a really thorough search, even to the point of making me strip off.

At Pale, where there was a marketplace, we stopped off and I bought five-kilogram packets of salt for Aza's family – salt was a much sought-after commodity – and some chocolate for Alida. I knew that if I asked the Jordanian UNMO to take this back for me he'd refuse, so I asked Boriša. Clearly he couldn't risk taking such a large amount, so I decided to hide the rest in the car – which, in hindsight, was very foolish of me, as it could have got the others into a great deal of trouble. I hid three or four of the packets in different places in the car and told Boriša where they were. I'm not sure what happened to the salt en route, as only a couple of kilograms reached Aza. In Sarajevo some photos I'd put in for developing were waiting for me, so I gave those, too, to Boriša to take back to Aza.

I also talked to a chap I knew from the international bar, who worked for the UN and knew what was what. Tomislav, a local Bosnian Serb who spoke five languages, was both very intelligent and completely foolhardy. I'd been told that, in the course of his work, he sometimes visited Zepa, and that in his vehicle there was a compartment where a person might hide. I had hopes of Tomislav. So I found him and broached the subject. 'No, no, no,' he said. 'Don't even think about it.'

Then he got up from his desk and turned the stereo up. I didn't realise until afterwards what he was doing, although many people working for the UN had expressed fears about being bugged. Against this musical background he told me that such a plan was feasible but much too risky; if we were caught all those involved would be shot.

'What other way is there?'

'As far as I can see, none at all,' he said. 'You're stuck.'

I'd thought he might at least have been able to make suggestions or provide contacts. If Tomislav was so discouraging, the future didn't seem at all promising.

Around that time, Sarajevo was in one of its more dangerous phases and most of the planes had been turned around. This left a large group of us all trying to get on one last flight. I reached the airport with my gear and waited there all day. The weather was freezing; the cold crept up through my boots, and the waiting room was dark and dismal. It was a long, horrible day; I was tired, cold and overwhelmed by too many thoughts and emotions.

When finally I got a seat on the plane, Joseph wanted to buy it from me. He was also supposed to be flying out that day, home to his family on leave. I said I had to be at my new sector the next day and 'work comes first'. I was desperate to go, to leave the last forty-eight hours behind me. Later I felt bad about my attitude because Joseph ended up being caught in Sarajevo for two weeks before he could get another flight out.

I went to Sector North, where Sergey and Pat were in charge, to the Croat side, to a small town called Sisak, which was on the Krajina border. I spent about a month there, doing the same job we'd been doing in Zepa except that these were Croat checkpoints and Croat soldiers. We were patrolling the UNprotected areas – the 'pink zones', we called them. Sometimes we patrolled late at night, trying to catch the Croats moving troops or equipment.

Because Sisak was only about an hour's drive from our headquarters in Zagreb, I went there quite often and would take with me a letter to Aza, enclosed in an envelope addressed to Jos. The Serbs would have noticed any mail addressed to Aza, but were unlikely to open letters with Jos's name on them. As an added precaution, I'd make up a return address in Holland or somewhere for the back of the envelope.

I would put the letter in the UN system's Sarajevo box. From Sarajevo it would be picked up by the supplies patrol from Zepa, then Jos would secretly pass it to Aza. The whole process could take a month or even two, because there were so many variables: flights from Zagreb might be cancelled, the road from Zepa might be impassable after heavy snow...

Now and again I'd run into one of the Zepa UNMOs who was at the headquarters, passing through or on leave. 'Do you know Aza? How is she?' It was so good to have news of her. One of them took a letter back with him, but many observers weren't prepared to smuggle letters for anyone in case they got caught.

Aza wrote back to me using the same kind of delivery system. I had made friends with some of the local interpreters and they would translate her letters for me. Indira, who had often done me the same favour in Sarajevo, and worked for the UN, had now been moved to Zagreb. This had been done through unofficial channels by a colonel for whom she used to work. It was an uncertain arrangement, since she was Muslim and Zagreb was in the Croat area. (Later she was to lose her job, for that very reason.) On my trips to Zagreb I'd drop in to see Indira. Among other things, we talked about Aza's passport, which was Yugoslav and therefore possibly obsolete. Indira said that Sanela had already applied for a Bosnian passport, and perhaps Aza would have to have one too. When I asked around, I was assured that a Yugoslav passport would no longer be accepted.

One of Indira's contacts happened to work at the Bosnian embassy in Zagreb, so she talked to him and reported back to me the next time I called in. The contact thought he might be able to help, so Indira and I went to the embassy to see him. Under his instructions, I filled out a couple of forms, paid him 130 deutschmarks and showed him Aza's passport. He looked at it and asked for the passport photos. 'Oh Brent,' I thought, 'you're an idiot – did you think he was just going to rip the old photo out and re-use it?'

Back to square one. I bought a roll of film and posted it to Jos with a letter asking him to please take a roll of passport-type photos of Aza as soon as possible.

After a month I was moved to Topusko, in the Krajina, which was considerably further from Zagreb. Almost as soon as I arrived in the town I was told of other Kiwis living there, so I rushed off to look them up. One was Greg Harris, a civilian who worked in the UN kitchen, and rented a flat in town; I moved into the flat below Greg's, so we saw a good deal of each other. To my utter amazement, the other Kiwi was Don Lough from Christchurch, who used to play cricket in the Christchurch Boys' High first eleven when I was playing for St Andrew's. Don was administration officer for our sector. Greg and Don had been nicknamed by the French UNMOs 'Rainbow' and 'Warrior'. Then Kevin Dudley turned up in town for New Year's Eve so the four of us got together, formed a Kiwi drinking team and had a good night. (Kevin and Julian Tangaere were the soldiers with whom I'd travelled over at the beginning of our mission.) It seemed quite bizarre that four Kiwis should turn up in a smallish town in Serb-occupied Croatia.

Whereas Topusko was on the Serb side of the border, Sector North covered both Croat and Serb territory.

Sergey Turganov was the senior military observer and Pat was his deputy, so I, as operations officer, was third in the chain of command. Under us, we had about sixty to seventy UNMOs in teams positioned throughout the area, the bulk of them on the Serb side of the border. Although many of those people were higher in rank than me, they were working beneath me; this was one of the peculiarities of the UN system.

As operations officer, I was responsible for co-ordinating tasks or activities in our area. When, for example, the UN organised a peace agreement that depended on a major withdrawal of weapons, Sector North had to monitor all the arms being removed from the front line between Croatia and the Krajina. It was my job to collect up all the information and compile it into the daily sitrep. This meant dealing with both sides and attending various meetings. But most of my time was spent keeping track of what the various teams were doing and how well they were doing it. With my own car, I had a lot more flexibility than before. The job was mainly paperwork – the desk job from which I had been trying to escape! – but at least it gave me some influence in that sector. On top of that, twice a week I had to hand-deliver what we called our 'intelligence summaries' to the senior operations officer in Zagreb. That was my chance to send off my letters and consult with Indira on the continuing passport saga.

It was a couple of months before Aza's passport photos arrived. In the meantime the man at the embassy had told Indira that I should go back and see him. I was told that he wasn't allowed to give me a passport without written authorisation from Aza and a stamped police clearance. So I sent off a letter to Aza explaining all this, again asking her to act as quickly as possible.

When I had the film developed, the photos were like

family snapshots of Aza standing in the snow. Indira and I took them to a photo lab to have one enlarged and manipulated into a semblance of a passport photo. The woman there did the best she could, and made some copies. I rushed these to the embassy and was told to return when I had the documentation from Aza. I waited and waited. I had a leave trip back to New Zealand in March and took the spare photos with me on the flight home. In Christchurch I explained my situation to an immigration officer and learned that I must first fill in a sponsorship form. After that we'd need to apply for a visitor's visa. Both involved a wad of forms which I took back with me to Topusko.

At this time, too, I made what turned out to be a very smart move. I left half of the passport photos in New Zealand. I knew that I'd have to apply for visas and they always required photos, so I left some behind just in case I lost the others or something else went wrong.

Straight after he took those photos for me, Jos had left the Zepa mission area and been replaced as team leader by Tom, a man we didn't know. But Jos schooled him up: 'There's this Kiwi chap and this young woman, and here's what you have to do...' So, even though he didn't know me, Tom took over smuggling our letters. I was immensely grateful for his help.

Time was passing and the papers from Aza still hadn't arrived. I had been posted to a mission in Belgrade and was due to leave on 1 April, which was rapidly approaching. From Belgrade in the east I was unlikely to visit Zagreb, which was up in the north-west. On my very last trip to Zagreb before I left for Belgrade Aza's letter arrived with both documents enclosed. Reprieved! I tried a number of times to ring the embassy contact but he wasn't there. Nor was Indira home. But this might be my last opportunity to get to the embassy, so off I went.

On my previous visits I had gone with Indira, and had been wearing my UN uniform. This time I was in civilian clothes, and on my own. There was always a queue of people outside the embassy door. There were so many Muslim refugees in Croatia all wanting passports to get out. I strode straight to the front of the line, banged on the door and handed in the papers from Aza. I was sent upstairs, quite respectfully, to an area where another group of people was milling around while the names were being read out of those whose passports were ready. Almost at once I heard her name, or at least heard the 'Aza' part. Pressing up against the office window, I could see that the teller was holding the forms I'd just handed in. *Yes!* I thought, I've finally got it.

It didn't have her signature yet, but at least we now had a legitimate Bosnian passport. From that moment on, Aza's passport went everywhere with me; I wore it strapped to my body. Getting it had been such a massive hurdle, and I knew I could never have managed it without Indira. A New Zealander turning up wanting to get hold of a Bosnian passport? They'd have marched me straight out the door. So now I had the passport, I had a sponsorship form from the New Zealand Immigration Department, and I had visa applications for New Zealand and Britain. The administration side was in motion. There were also some developments on the practical side.

It had taken a while for me to get to know Sergey. We didn't see a lot of him at Sisak; he only came about once a week and he would spend most of his days out talking with the local commanders and his nights out drinking with Pat. Initially, I wasn't operations officer. That position was held by a Dutchman who didn't approve of Sergey's and Pat's carousing ways. They could go out drinking all night and still do their job the next morning, but that Dutchman was a thorn in their side. So when he was posted out, I was quickly moved into his job.

At first my motives for getting close to Sergey were rather suspect, in that I was thinking of Aza, but I genuinely liked the man. He was practical and active, with a good outlook on life. He was only in his early thirties but, owing to hard living, he looked considerably older. All the Russian soldiers seemed to live hard, but Sergey lived harder than most.

He had a flat and a car and a wife (his second) and children back in Moscow, whom he kept 'safe' in his absence by paying protection money to the local mafia. An observer's salary was a lot of money in Russia, so the mafia made sure it got spread around. In an effort to make up the deficit, Sergey invested his US dollars at home at fifteen per cent interest a *month*. He was a man who had been places and done exciting things. He spoke three languages fluently – Serbo-Croat and English, as well as his native Russian. He'd been trained in intelligence and had worked in a special unit – not, he said, the KGB, though I was never totally convinced about that.

Eventually Sergey, Pat and I would go drinking and partying together. We got along well, and I discovered Sergey had his own romantic problems. He was at this stage infatuated with one of our interpreters, a girl called Diana, whose Serb boyfriend was something of a local hero in his own town. (He was later killed in a mysterious car crash) The boyfriend was also a friend of Sergey's, so Sergey was trying to spend as much time as possible with Diana, without the boyfriend knowing. Diana was only about nineteen, and impressionable, pretty but empty-headed. Sergey would pick her up from her parents' house where she lived and sneak around with her. They'd slept together only once and afterwards she'd regretted it and, to Sergey's distress, said, 'No more.'

Pat became involved in all this because Diana made him her confidante. Pat, too, was married with young children, and he was only being kind to Diana, but Sergey became suspicious, angry and jealous. Greg, too, was keen on Diana. When he took her out one night, Sergey chased them down the road and rammed into the back of Greg's car.

I could see that Sergey was as obsessed with Diana as I had been with Aza while I was in Zepa. This thought just depressed me because I felt that since then I'd achieved nothing towards helping her to escape. I'd lie awake at night hatching ridiculous plans: Shall I fly a helicopter over from Italy? I was beginning to think that the whole idea was just not possible and that I ought to forget it.

But one night, when we were drinking at a local bar called Bonnie & Clyde's, Sergey asked about my love life. I explained about Aza.

'It's hopeless,' I said. 'She's trapped in this Muslim enclave and there's no way of getting her out.'

'What do you mean – no way?'

'Well,' I said, 'you know the situation.'

'Yes,' said Sergey, 'but what you don't understand is that General Mladic is a personal friend of mine. I know people who can take care of these problems. It's easy.'

'You're joking!' I told myself it was just the drink talking, especially when Sergey said it was easy. It wasn't easy, I knew that for sure.

'I'll have to call a friend of mine in Sarajevo, but I don't have his number on me.'

Despite myself, I felt excited. I couldn't get Aza out through the official channels, so unofficial means seemed at least to offer a ray of hope. I said no more about it that night, but a couple of weeks later I mentioned the matter to Sergey again. 'Okay,' he said, 'we'll go and make a call.'

He rang the Lukavica headquarters in Sarajevo to speak to a Major Kušic´ – I remembered having met him during my few days at Lukavica barracks – who was one of the Bosnian Serb liaison officers there.

Sergey began talking to Kušic´ in Serbo-Croat, and by now I could pick up a little of the language. He was saying, 'I've got this friend...' and 'You know we can do this.'

The major told him, 'For you, my friend, anything.'

Sergey put down the phone. 'Yes, Kiwi, no worries.'

I thought, 'There has to be more to it than this!' I was shaking my head – no, no, no.

'Yes,' he said. 'Too right it will happen.'

I still couldn't believe it. 'So what next?'

'Give me a ring in a couple of weeks and we'll talk about that.'

It *was* going to happen! I still didn't know how, nor did I believe it could be as simple as Sergey was making it sound, but there were people who could make it happen, and I knew the right ones! I went back into the bar, punching the air. *Yes!*

The barmaid at Bonnie & Clyde's, where we were regulars, said, 'Kiwi, why are you so happy?' She and her workmates spoke a little English and I managed some Serbo-Croat.

I said, 'I'm going to shout the bar', and I bought a round of drinks for the fifteen or twenty people present.

I knew a lot of the locals at this stage, who liked Sergey, Pat and me because we talked with them. Now they were asking, 'What are you celebrating, Kiwi?'

'Life,' I said.

This happened during my last few days in the Krajina, so when the passport also came through, I began to feel cautiously optimistic.

The British, Canadian and New Zealand observers seemed to end up at the UN headquarters in Belgrade because we spoke English and could work the computers, which together amounted to what they called 'good communication skills', although all the paperwork was actually rather boring. So Belgrade became my next posting.

When I first arrived, I shared a flat with a British UNMO called Captain Robert Dansey. Robert was coming towards the end of his time in Belgrade when I arrived, and his new posting was to Sarajevo, which, of course, controlled the Zepa mission. By then we were good friends and he knew all about Aza, so I suggested I should try to organise for him to join the team in Zepa. 'I need a contact on the inside.'

'Mate,' said Robert, 'I'm only too willing to help.'

So I rang my fellow Kiwi, Julian Tangaere, who was at that stage operations officer in Sarajevo, and who knew how much I was in love with Aza, to ask if he could have Robert posted to Zepa. 'It will be done,' said Julian.

So Robert went off to Zepa and introduced himself to Aza. He would send me faxes telling me about how things were with her and her family. This communication meant a great deal to me, isolated in Belgrade – and not only from Aza, but also from Sergey.

Although it was possible to put a call through from Belgrade to the Krajina, that call had to travel on a satellite system through Zagreb and the lines were very bad. After a few unsuccessful attempts I finally got through to Sergey, who told me that I would have speak to Kušic´ myself, because Sarajevo was closer to Belgrade and the lines were better.

I had already been able to organise a fake UN ID card for Aza, thanks to the help of the local interpreters. (I'd introduced myself to them when I arrived and, as usual, they'd responded well to those who made an effort to speak their language.) Interpreters had yellow cards, which meant that you were local. With one of those, Aza would be quizzed as to her ethnicity and where she was going, but with a white UN ID card you could go anywhere in the mission area.

Acquiring the right sort of white plastic card had not been easy. It had been necessary to send away to another sector, where someone had access to the correct card, and the whole process had taken a long time.

Some of the men in the UN system had tried to design ID cards on their computers – and some of these had worked. Another chap in Sarajevo had done this too, making two white ID cards for a couple so that they and their child could escape to Italy. The couple arrived at the airport with their baby hidden in a brown shopping bag and presented themselves, and their false ID cards, at the air movements window. The cards were accepted and they left Sarajevo for freedom in Italy.

There was a great deal of this falsifying of documents going on in Bosnia. In some cases, senior UN officials were bribed. Secret intelligence work among UN officials was not uncommon either. A number of embassies put pressure on their nationals working for the UN to provide information, which in turn aroused the suspicions of the Serb authorities. I myself was followed and questioned. One day, when I was coming out of McDonalds, I saw someone just leaning against a car, watching me; on another occasion, I was almost run off the road. My phone was certainly bugged – I could clearly hear the clicking sound. Belgrade was a scary place and the atmosphere increased my fear about Aza being caught.

Once I had the card, I began to add the necessary details – Aza's photograph, a false name which I typed in, a forged signature. It was all highly illegal, but I was sure we'd have to use that card at some stage. And it would need to be laminated, so I went to the office where they kept the small portable laminating machine and said, 'My bloody UN ID card's come to bits. I need to borrow your machine to relaminate it.'

'You know where it's kept,' the woman said. 'Help yourself.'

But first the card needed the official red UN stamp, and this was going to prove tricky. The chief administration officer in Belgrade kept the stamp locked in his office and there was no way I could get in there and use it. But there was another stamp down in the operations officer's room, which wasn't part of the UNMO system. However, this one used blue ink, so I had to get hold of that one – and change the ink.

A British friend worked in the communications centre where the keys were kept, and I knew the operations officers didn't work at weekends. So, on a Saturday morning, when the British chap and I were both at work, I snatched the keys to the operations office, ran down and grabbed the stamp. Just as I came out and was locking the door behind me, one of the operations officers turned the corner. I did a fast about-turn and raced back to return the keys before he got there to sign them out.

Hoping that the operations officer wasn't at that moment looking around for it, I took the stamp back to my own office. I'd lined up some red ink and some blue, so I just had to clean off the blue ink, pour some of the red on to a wad of toilet paper to make a blotting pad, press down the stamp and stamp Aza's ID card. Done. I cleaned off the red ink, replaced it with blue, borrowed the key again and returned both the stamp and the key.

That night I went out on the town, not returning home until early the next morning, so I wasn't feeling too well the following day. I got out the laminator, plugged it in and let it warm up. Putting the card inside the plastic cover, I fed it into the machine and waited for the finished product to emerge. It didn't. The machine had eaten the card.

I couldn't leave the card in the machine to be discovered – somehow I had extricate it. I fed my own ID in behind the first card and, sure enough, it pushed the other card out. But it was now just a crumpled mess. I wanted to cry. All that time, risk and effort had been chewed up in a couple of seconds.

I felt the same kind of helpless fury I had experienced when my car was burgled. I had begun taking lessons in Serbo-Croat at a local school, and one day when I returned to my car after class I found a window was smashed and the bag containing my spare uniform had gone. The uniform didn't matter, but in that bag there was also a folder that had held my spare passport, all of Aza's letters, the sponsorship form, the visa application forms with her photos on them, and the spare photos. Everything had gone.

There was nothing I could do but start all over again. I quickly made a call to New Zealand. 'Mum, I need you to go to immigration and get me another sponsorship form and more visa application forms and please send me those spare photographs.' Mail from New Zealand took only a couple of weeks. I was at least thankful that Aza's passport was still safely strapped to my body.

Robert had some good friends and contacts in Belgrade, and in those first weeks before he left for Zepa I'd got to know them. One was Colonel Pat Crandell, the Canadian defence attaché. Knowing my situation, he told me that he was going to be in London for a few days and was there anything he could do for me there? I asked him if he would please go to the Immigration Department of the New Zealand embassy and have a word with them. I'd organised a British visa for Aza, but the last thing we needed was New Zealand visa problems if and when we got to Britain. So Pat Crandell did that, and it made a great difference. One way or another, there were so many people who went out of their way to help me with my plans.

I was very nervous about ringing Sergey's friend, Kušic´. I didn't know how he'd react – he might have forgotten all about me and my problem. I had to force myself to make that call, but when I said who I was he remembered both me and the situation. He said it was too dangerous to talk on the phone: I would have to go to Sarajevo and see him.

Soon after this, travelling from one part of the mission area to another was banned, but at that stage it was still possible, although you were expected to have a very good reason for going to hot spots such as Sarajevo. I was sure I could get there, though. I was owed a favour by my boss, who had just been to Sarajevo himself for a naughty weekend. He was married but also had a girlfriend, and he'd asked me to cover for him if his superiors in Zagreb rang. I'd done that.

Now I told him, 'I need to go to Sarajevo.'

'Just don't let the SMO see you.' That particular senior military observer, who had taken over in Sarajevo when I was leaving, was known as The Screaming Skull. If he saw me he'd know who I was and want to know what I was there for.

Robert Dansey, having spent about a month in Zepa, had returned to Belgrade on a week's leave. I'd planned to drive him back to Zagreb, and catch a plane from there to Sarajevo. To travel by air through the UN system you made an authorised application and seats were allotted on a first-in first-served basis. I signed those forms myself, which was only marginally illegal since my boss had said I could go to Sarajevo. So Robert and I drove to Zagreb, only to find that all flights to Sarajevo that day were full. But we stayed at the airport just in case someone failed to show up, and my luck was in – we got on the last flight.

I stayed that night at Sanela's flat, because I needed to keep out of sight. Kušic´ knew I was arriving that Friday, but we hadn't arranged to meet until Sunday. On the Saturday morning I got a call from Kevin McElvoy, a fellow New Zealander at the Sarajevo headquarters, who had just taken a brisk phone call from Kušic´: 'Tell Brent Kiwi to come and see me right now.' Kevin was a friend of Sanela's. I was extremely lucky that he happened to take that call.

I wasn't prepared to meet Kušic´ so soon. In Zagreb I had bought cartons of Marlboro cigarettes and a couple of bottles of whisky for Kušic´, to smooth the way; I had those, but no transport. At this stage the city of Sarajevo was like a fortress. The Muslim front lines surrounded the inner city while the outer suburbs, exclusively Serb or Muslim, were separated by open fields lethal with mines and snipers. UN flights and UN vehicles were the only things that were being allowed in and out. Lukavica was only about a ten-minute drive away, but in order to reach it we had to pass through those Muslim lines.

I managed to get hold of a jeep and drove to the Lukavica headquarters. Kušić came to the door to meet me and I gave him the whisky and cigarettes. He ushered me through a side door, offered me *rakija* and left me there with another man – the Bosnian Serb colonel, Goran, who'd shared his office during my short time in Lukavica – saying he'd be with me in a minute.

When he rejoined us, Kušić asked me if I'd prefer the conversation to be held in English or Serbo-Croat. I opted for English and he agreed but said, 'I know you understand exactly what I'm saying when I speak Serbo-Croat.' This wasn't quite true but there was no point in protesting – the Serbs always suspected that those of us who could speak a little of their language understood far more than we let on. We sat there while Kušić did all the talking.

'Right,' he said. 'As Sergey would have told you, Kiwi, with me you don't get anything for nothing.'

Goran said something to Kušić, then left the room.

'Your situation is understandable,' Kušić assured me. 'A young man comes to the country and falls in love. I don't have a problem with the fact that she's Muslim. You can't help that, you're just young and in love. I will help you out if you will help me out.'

I waited.

'Here is what I want,' he said. 'There are two people inside the city. I want them smuggled out and brought to me. Then you will have your girl from Zepa.'

He was asking a great deal of me. A UN observer smuggling people out of a city was going completely against the rules. At the same time I knew it could be done, and had been done. I also knew – and I'm sure that was a factor at work here – that these two men had worked closely with Kiwis who had come before me.

Kušić then refilled our glasses and grew very convivial. The two of us went off to lunch together, drank some more and talked. Kušić gave me a piece of paper. 'This is the first person we want. This is where he lives. That is his phone number.'

There was no sense of urgency. I had the impression he was expecting me to go away and do it within the next two or three weeks.

'If you give me these two you will have the girl, no problem at all. I guarantee it.'

I believed him. I knew he saw it as a business deal. He gave me a couple of false interpreter ID cards with random photos, in case we needed to use them.

By then we'd drunk quite a lot of *rakija*. I said I had to go but I'd be in touch. Back in the car, I headed back through the front lines to Sarajevo, thinking, 'I can't do this, it's smuggling.' If I got caught I'd either be shot by the Muslims or shot by the Serbs or spat out sideways by the system. It would be an international smuggling incident. When I looked at it that way, and thought of the possible consequences, the whole notion was terrifying.

I knew of two possible routes out of the city. The first was through the airport; the Muslim checkpoint there was casual, and then you went into the French part within the airport, and out through the Serb checkpoints. Once I'd reached them I'd be set, because I'd have a Serb sitting in the back! If the fake IDs were examined by Muslim or French soldiers I'd be in deep trouble because the photos wouldn't match, but, to my advantage, UNMOs usually had an interpreter with them, and the French soldiers were often young conscripts and not very bright.

The second possible route was to go out through an area called Dobrinja. I went and did a recce of the Dobrinja checkpoint. For some reason it wasn't manned at the time, and soldier activity seemed low. So that remained an option. Driving back, I worked on a plan.

Back at headquarters I swapped the jeep for a GMC, an armoured vehicle with tinted windows. I organised this through one of my friends at the base without saying what I was up to. It was risky for me even to be seen around the Sarajevo HQ, and I had just stepped into the corridor when I saw the senior military officer – The Screaming Skull – heading towards me. I ducked into an office and he went on by.

I drove back to Sanela's flat in the GMC, and I got her to ring the number Kušic´ had given us. I arranged to meet the man at a certain corner, then drove up and down the street until someone came along and stopped in the general area. Pulling in alongside him, I wound down my window and checked that he was the right person.

'Right, get in the car.' I pulled my seat forward. He jumped in the back and I wound up the tinted glass window.

I drove around while he told me something about himself. He spoke no English so we had to make do with my pidgin Serbo-Croat. The man was a Bosnian Serb in his mid- to late twenties. His family, separated from him at the start of the war, had fled to Austria but he'd been forcibly 'conscripted' by the Muslim militia, who were making him dig trenches on the front lines. This ploy, used by both sides, meant that if or when these men were shot, it was by their own people. He was living in constant fear for his life and was under regular surveillance in a flat in a Muslim part of the city.

'Right,' I said. 'You're going to leave, and we're going now.'

His face lit up. I don't think he could believe it.

'Are you carrying your passport and ID?'

He was. I gave him one of the fake ID cards. 'Hang this around your neck, and if you're questioned let me do the talking.'

I'd decided to take the Dobrinja route. I was terrified, and could feel the adrenalin pumping. We passed a few soldiers on the way, but when we came within sight of the Muslim checkpoint we could see that the sentry-box was unattended. I decided that if we got to within fifty metres of the box and then were waved down, we'd make a run for it. The vehicle was bullet-proof and once we were through that checkpoint we'd be safely in Serb territory. I cruised along, hardly daring to breathe, but no one stepped out. I drove through. It was that easy.

When I reached Lukavica, Kušić and Goran were astounded. 'You've done it already?' Of course they were delighted; they made a phone call and the mayor of Lukavica turned up. I was ceremonially presented with a bottle of *rakija*, which everyone signed, and they took some photos. A happy occasion. Then they gave me the name of the second man.

Off I went back into the city, to ring the number I'd been given. But when I asked to speak to the person concerned I was told he didn't live there. I drove back to report this to Kušić. 'Then he is just not answering to that name,' he said.

Kušić made the call. 'Yes, he is there. It's okay.'

Apparently the man had gone underground and hadn't shown his face for months. He believed the Muslims were intent on killing him. He wasn't a soldier; I don't know what he'd done or was supposed to have done.

I had only just reached the arranged meeting place

when the man appeared, as if out of nowhere, and climbed straight into the back of my vehicle. I turned and hung the other ID card around his neck.

'Right,' I said. 'We're leaving now. Are you ready?'

'Oh God, yes,' he whispered.

This time we took the airport route. At the Muslim checkpoint they gave us a wave, but the French stopped us. I don't speak French but I smiled and they laughed and looked in at my ID card but, luckily, not too closely. My passenger just pointed to his – he looked nothing like the photo on it – and then the Frenchmen flagged us on.

I'd done it! I delivered this man to Lukavica and drank a few glasses of *rakija*. I was high on adrenalin and relief. 'I've done it – Aza's almost on her way.'

Then Kušic´ said, 'What about doing just one more?'

'Yes,' I heard myself saying. 'Oh yes! No worries.'

This time I was given not a phone number but a name and a rather vague address. So I picked up Sanela and drove to the area and began asking people where the man lived. This in itself was likely to arouse suspicion; had I been sober, I would never have involved myself in this third rescue. But the man had heard from Kus•ic and turned up, very excited at the prospect of leaving – his mother, he told us, was seriously ill in another town. When he asked how much he could take with him, we said just one small bag. But this posed the problem of how and where we would meet him. People were already looking at us with some interest. If he got into the car carrying a bag, it would be obvious what was going on. It was common knowledge that some UN personnel would smuggle people out for a price. Word was that for 10,000 deutschmarks, there were French soldiers who would get you to an overseas country.

We arranged to meet the man again in a fairly deserted area. Sanela decided that she would come with me to Lukavica. It was dangerous for a Muslim girl to cross to the Serb side, but Sanela was known to Goran. Having given the man time to pack his bags, we met him as arranged. We took the first route, through Dobrinja, and once again all went smoothly, apart from a hiccup on the Serb side, when one of the checkout soldiers became difficult. We got him to call Kušic´ and Goran and he quickly changed his tune.

At Lukavica they'd put on a big meal for us and there was more drinking and celebration. Kušic´ asked when I wanted them to get Aza. I said I'd call him next week from Belgrade and let him know. This was at the end of May. I said it would probably be within the next couple of weeks.

When I woke up the next morning, I could hardly believe what I'd done. I was just waiting for the repercussions, for someone to start wondering why I was in Sarajevo and what I'd been up to. It had been a dangerous business, and it wasn't just my neck I was risking, but also Sanela's. There was no way I could ever have done it without her help.

Back in Sarajevo, I saw Robert, who was returning to Zepa that day and would give Aza the good news. We talked about which date I should give Kušic´, and worked out a code to use when sending each other messages. Next day I drove to Belgrade. On that journey, the reality of what I'd done and what it meant finally sank in and suddenly I felt uncertain. Should I really go through with this? Was it the right thing to do? It wasn't too late to change my mind, but it soon would be.

Yet I couldn't bear the thought of Aza rotting away in Zepa and I had promised to get her out. How could I let her down?

From Belgrade I faxed Robert to confirm the date: 9 June. It was only ten days away. We agreed I would ring him again on the 7th to give him the final details. I rang Kušić and told him. And then I was hit by a great surge of doubt. Getting Aza into Serbia was only the first step; she still wouldn't be safe, she still wouldn't be free. And if I did succeed in getting her out, how would she feel living in an English-speaking country when she didn't speak English, when even she and I had trouble communicating?

Did we even really know each other? We had spent perhaps a grand total of sixty minutes absolutely alone together. We'd kissed twice. What if the relationship didn't work out? Aza would be trapped in an enemy country with no way of returning home. I worried, too, about the effect it would have on her family, who not only loved her, but depended on her.

I considered all those things, and then I thought back to my time in Zepa. The nights when I lay awake in bed wanting to be with her. The hours I spent just thinking about her – obsessed, besotted. And I saw that I loved her very much and that this part – getting her out of Bosnia – would be the biggest problem we'd ever have to face. If we could overcome this hurdle, we could face anything else the future might throw at us. We would just have to take life one step at a time.

Having pushed aside all my doubts, I suddenly had something else to worry about. On 5 or 6 June a memo arrived on my desk advising that the UN's chief military observer would be doing a tour of the mission areas on the 13th. I knew this would definitely include Sarajevo, but he wouldn't have time to visit all the teams.

'Please,' I thought, 'don't let him be going to Zepa!' I felt fairly sure that, even by going to Sarajevo, he would come to hear about Aza. It would be four days after she'd left, and smuggling out a Muslim girl would cause much interest. I became resigned to the fact that I was almost certain to be found out one way or another. I only had about two months left to serve but I couldn't expect to be lucky enough to complete them. I had a week's leave due, so I arranged to take it from the 9th so Aza and I could spend that time together.

I thought that Kušic´ might just organise the checkpoint clearances and have me drive to Zepa to collect Aza, so I started looking around for a diesel vehicle – petrol was harder to come by – that would cover the distance without refuelling. I arranged a swap with another team for a four-wheel-drive Cherokee, and acquired a couple of spare tanks of diesel fuel.

On the 7th I rang Kušic´ as arranged. We agreed that Robert would take Aza to the outskirts of Zepa, where Kušic´ had arranged for a man called Dragan, driving a VW Golf, to meet them and head up through Bosnia to a bridge on the Bosnia-Serbia border. All I had to do was rendezvous with them there.

It sounded easy enough. The next day I drove from Belgrade down through Serbia to that bridge, just to familiarise myself with the route. Robert was expecting to deliver Aza to me on the outskirts of Zepa, so that made me panic a little. We didn't have a capsat machine in our section, so I had to race down to the European Community monitors at Hotel Yugoslavia and ask to use theirs. The man there was co-operative – I'd used their machine before.

I quickly typed out a message to Robert, which I couldn't really code in case it just confused him. I typed: *Robert, I can't make that next rendezvous. I am looking forward to seeing you though later on that day. Don't worry, a good friend of ours, Dragan, will turn up. Expect to see him in his VW Golf at that prearranged time. Everything is okay. He will look after you. See you in a couple of days.*

That message went on capsat to Zepa, so who knows how many UNMOs saw it.

I think I asked Robert to acknowledge receipt; at this stage I was becoming really anxious about the possibility of a hitch in the arrangements. By the morning of 9 June I had convinced myself that something would go wrong and Aza would not arrive.

Branco, my Belgrade landlord, decided to come with me in the Cherokee. He seemed almost as excited as I was. The meeting at the bridge was scheduled for two p.m., and it was a two-and-a-half to three-hour drive, so we left before eleven. I was terribly tense, and I guess it was obvious because Branco kept asking me if I was all right.

I wasn't. And my state was not improved by the number of toll gates we had to pass through. I'd been in those parts long enough to have grown very weary of the endless rules and regulations, and road taxes were especially infuriating because UNMOs would be charged ten or fifteen times more than the locals.

At the toll gate where we turned off the highway, the chap in the booth was friendly. Branco was chatting away to him while I handed over the ten deutschmarks. By mistake he gave the same amount back as change. As we drove off, I realised what had happened.

'You'll have to go back and return it,' Branco said.

'Oh, forget it. They're daylight robbers.' In the rear-view mirror I could see that the man had discovered his mistake and was trying to attract my attention. I knew I should go back but I was so on edge, so focused on reaching the bridge that, although we had plenty of time, even a small delay seemed unbearable.

'No,' said Branco, 'we have to go back. They'll make him repay it out of his wages.'

This made me feel guilty, so I turned around and gave the man the money. He was delighted, so I was glad that Branco had insisted.

We reached the bridge and the towns of Mali Zvornik and Zvornik, which nestle either side of the big Drina River that winds through Serbia and Bosnia, passing close to Zepa. Here the river served as the border between the two countries and the bridge was quite a long one. On our side there was a Serb checkpoint and, on the other side, a Bosnian Serb checkpoint. Even though they were on the same side, the Serbs weren't keen to be flooded with Bosnian Serb refugees, and they certainly didn't want Muslims, so they were vigilant about checking IDs.

We parked the car and waited. By now I was horribly nervous. Branco kept saying, 'It's going to be all right, Kiwi. Just relax. It's going to be all right.' It was reassuring having Branco there; he reminded me of my father.

A couple of UN convoys rolled through. In the French one there must have been forty vehicles – big trucks, personnel carriers... We sat there waving and waiting. Time ticked on to two o'clock. We were straining to see every approaching VW Golf. I wished I'd asked for the colour; there were red ones, blue ones, white ones. With every car that came over that bridge my heart went springboarding into my mouth.

There weren't that many vehicles coming from Bosnia, just one every few minutes: 'There's a car... it's a VW Golf... it might be her... no, there's only one person in it...' After forty-five minutes of this, Branco was in the same state as me. He would go to the shop and buy a couple of beers, come back, drink his as he paced around, unable to keep still. I forced a couple of beers down, but was in no mood for drinking.

An hour went by, then an hour and a half. I began to feel utterly despondent. They weren't coming. Branco's wife was at home preparing a celebration dinner, all for nothing. Aza wasn't going to get through. We might as well jump into the car and drive home.

'No,' said Branco, 'we'll give it a little longer.'

chapter nine

The Escape

How could I leave Alida? In all my life she was the one I was closest to. I had always thought that everywhere I went, I would take her; she would be with me. She was like part of me. Everything she learned, she learned from me. Everything she did, she did for me; she was my little self. How could I leave her?

That night, when Brent left with Joseph to walk to the car, my little sister and I were both crying. As we went to our bedroom in the neighbours' house, Alida was asking me a million questions: 'Will he come back? When? What's going to happen?' And the more she asked, the more I cried.

Our blanket-covered window faced out to where their car was, so we could hear from the continuous revving that the vehicle was stuck. Looking out, I saw someone walking back towards our house; I thought it was Brent and that we'd have another chance to say goodbye through the window. But it was Joseph, who'd forgotten his hat. He said goodbye again but I couldn't make my throat reply. My father had gone out to help and soon I could hear the car moving. From another window I watched it on the road, picking up speed. I thought, 'This is the last time I will ever see him.'

The next morning I tried my hardest to look as if everything were normal. The last thing I needed was for my family to know how I felt and to start saying, 'How can you be so stupid? Put him out of your mind, he's gone forever.'

But that night Alida began talking about Brent and I started to cry again. I tried not to let her see, because then she would cry too. She loved Brent very much and had told me that, although she had always imagined that she and I would be together forever, if I would rather be with someone else she wouldn't mind as long as it was Brent.

But Brent had gone, and now the little voice in my head that had been nagging at me all along became very loud: *I told you it would be like this. You are stupid. What made you think this one was so special and different?* 'Okay,' I told the voice, 'he's gone, and that's that. I'll keep busy, I'll do lots of work outside.'

Then, three days after Brent left, I received a letter he'd written in Sarajevo. Jos dropped it off. That voice in my head had been saying, *Perhaps he was very bored*. But I didn't believe it. He was still thinking about me. He still loved me. I cried again, but this time from happiness. With the letter there was a photo of Brent in his air force uniform beside a helicopter, taken in Fiji. It wasn't the Brent I knew. That photo belonged to his life before he met me. I was glad to have it, yet it gave me a very odd feeling. In that photo it was his face, but it was also the face of a stranger. I kept it on my bedside table, protected by glass. My family saw Jos give me the letter so I pretended to be very casual about it. 'Oh, he's fine. He says...' And I told them what I thought they wanted to hear. In fact, I couldn't read it at all. It took me two nights with my little dictionary to translate it.

For twenty days I waited for another letter. It was snowing in the Krajina and everything had stopped. Our military observers would go into Sarajevo and collect the mail but there was nothing for me. Again the voice was talking to me: *That photo is the last you'll see of him. It was his way of saying goodbye.*

I would manage to act cheerful during the day, but at night Alida would talk about Brent and I'd start to cry – because perhaps he'd gone forever, or just because I missed him so much. Then my little sister would try so hard to cheer me up: 'He is gone but I will sing you a song.' And she would sing, '*Volim te budala mala...*' Brent used to say those words to me. '*Volim te budala mala*' – 'I love you, small fool.' And first thing in the mornings, when I opened my eyes, Alida would look across at me – 'I love you, small fool.'

Gradually I found that I could speak about Brent without dissolving into tears and then Alida and I had happy talks at night. We called them our bedtime stories. Her favourite story – the one she told me most often – was that one day Brent would come back in a helicopter and Alida and I would be waiting for him, our bags already packed and under our beds. When we saw the helicopter we would grab our bags and run to it. We'd jump in as soon as it landed, before our parents could catch us. 'And we'll fly away with Brent and all live happily ever after.'

Alida had it all planned. In New Zealand she would sleep in the same room as Brent and me.

'Darling, you can't.'

'Then I'll sleep in his sister's room, and when she gets married it will be my room.'

Alida knew her stories would eventually make me smile, and then she'd say, 'Can I kiss you now, okay?' It felt as if I were the little child and she was my big sister. Because she'd almost always been there when Brent and I were together she knew how much he meant to me. She understood exactly how I was feeling.

The nights were really the only chance I had to translate his letters. Sometimes during the day, when everyone else was busy, I'd sneak off to our bedroom and take up his latest letter, but within a few minutes my mother would be calling for me. And I would have liked to work on those letters in the daytime because at night I had only a small can of cooking oil and a wick. It was smelly and didn't give much light, and my dictionary was pocket-sized, with very small print.

When Alida was with me she would keep talking and asking questions, so I told her I wouldn't go to bed when she did unless she went straight to sleep. After that she would wheedle our parents to let her sleep in their bed until I was ready to retire, then ask me, 'Was I good?'

'Yes,' I'd say. 'Perfect.'

'Tomorrow night perhaps you'll let me come and watch you?'

So I'd give in and the next night she'd be lying there, watching.

'What does he say?'

'I don't know yet.'

'Can you see my name anywhere?'

'Yes.' He'd have sent her a big hug or a kiss.

'What does it say?'

'I can't tell you until I've translated the letter.'

I'd be aware of her waiting, trying to be patient, and then she'd fall asleep. When I woke next morning I'd see her big brown eyes on me, waiting for me to wake up.

'You're awake?'

'No,' I'd say, 'I need some more sleep.'

'First can you just tell me what he wrote?'

I was never quite sure I'd got it right. It was just a translation dictionary with everyday words and phrases; it didn't allow for the past tense or the way that a sentence should go together. All I could do was go through the letters word by word, looking them up and writing down the Bosnian equivalent, and often he'd used words that weren't there so I'd have to guess.

Sometimes I got the meaning completely wrong. In one letter he wrote: 'If the Serbs ever stop my letters from reaching you, don't ever imagine that means I've stopped thinking about you.' I thought he was saying that the Serbs were going to stop him sending letters. I was in tears, thinking, 'This is the last letter I'm going to get from him.' I believed this until Jos called in with another letter. He was with Boriša, and my parents weren't home so we could talk. When he asked if I'd managed to translate the last letter, I said there was one sentence I wasn't sure about – and, even thinking about it, my tears came. In fact, just seeing Jos would make me want to cry, and he knew that; sometimes he would almost be crying himself. Then he'd act hearty and pat me on the shoulder, 'How are you? Okay?'

Jos was so kind to me. From the time Brent left Jos would call around almost every second day. He told me I must be patient and that one day Brent and I would be together and happy. Now Jos said, 'Let Boriša translate it. Where's the letter?' I didn't want Boriša reading the letter, so I just copied down the sentence and gave him that. And when he translated it I knew I'd become upset over something that wasn't even there.

One letter would keep me happy for five days. It would

take me a couple of nights to translate it, then for the next three or four nights I would read it over and over. After five days I would be waiting for the next letter. I knew it might be as long as three weeks before it would arrive, but that didn't stop me hoping every day. I'd stay close to home in case someone came with a letter when I wasn't there.

If anyone connected with the UN team called in, I would widen my eyes at him in question. If there was no response I'd know it was just a visit, but if they opened their eyes wide in return it would mean yes. Then I would go up close to say hello so he could pass the letter out from under his jacket and I could slip it down the sleeve of my jersey. Sometimes it remained there for hours before I got a chance to look at it. I always wanted to open the letter while it was still daylight – I couldn't read it, but I liked to know how long it was, and therefore how soon I would know what it said.

Some of what Brent wrote concerned everyday things, but mostly the letters were romantic, saying lovely things that made me so happy. Once he wrote: 'I am twenty-five years old, and I will wait the next five or ten or fifty or one hundred years – however long it takes – to be with you.' That meant a lot because I was also waiting for him. It was all I could do.

At night, when I had read and reread his letters, I would write back to him. At first I tried to write them in simple words so that he could understand them without translation, but once I knew he had interpreters to translate them I could write what came into my head. Even then I was never sure that I'd managed to put on paper the way I really felt. I don't think that was possible.

I wanted to write to him every day, but I imagined him being deluged with letters he didn't have time to read, and restrained myself. I would smuggle the letters to Jos or one of the other soldiers. One day, after not having heard from Brent for a while, I received a letter saying he'd been in Austria on holiday, and he'd been hoping to find a letter waiting when he returned. He was so disappointed because he hadn't had a letter for some time. I was terribly upset, because I had written him letters; they hadn't arrived. I thought he might stop writing to me. I wrote him a letter to explain; I think it reached him the same time as all those missing letters.

Besides Alida, who was still just a child, I had two girlfriends in whom I confided. One was Amira, a Muslim girl of my own age. We'd been friends since school, and I could tell her anything and know she would never pass it on. She was the best friend anyone could have. She took a great interest in Brent's letters and our situation and never once questioned it. She could see that it was right for me, that he made me happy. When I'd translated the letters, I would read them to her.

Other people I knew would ask me about Brent. 'Has Kiwi gone, then?'

'Yes.'

'Have you heard from him?'

If I said no, they would give me an I-told-you-so look, so usually I'd say, 'Yes. Once or twice.'

'What does he have to say?'

'Oh, nothing much.'

I could see other boys were thinking that I was now available. 'She was obsessed with him, but now he's gone and it can be my turn.' But I had my letters, so why would I need them? To me those boys meant nothing, they didn't exist.

Miroslav, who had been a good friend to me and Brent, left Zepa suddenly – one day he was there and the next he was gone – and after that Boriša began calling in more and more on various pretexts. He would tell me how he, too, would soon be leaving. And how, if Brent had really cared for me, he could simply have taken me with him. He said we could have been married at the registry office in Zepa and I could have travelled as Brent's wife. I told him not to be stupid, that wasn't possible.

In our village winter was essentially a time of quiet waiting, so I was used to that. We would wait, each year, for spring. But for me spring was always a time of impatience and expectation. I would feel excitement and a longing – for *something*; I didn't know what.

At the beginning of spring, I had word from Brent that he was making me a new passport and there were things he needed. The first was photos: I must go to Zepa for Jos to take photographs of me. It was Jos's last day in the area and he would take the photos, then carry the film out with him and send it to Brent. I had to be there early in the morning, before he went on patrol, and without my parents knowing. It had snowed all that night but I was there by eight o'clock. Jos couldn't find a place inside to take the photos so we had to go outside, where there were masses of people because this was the day the Red Cross food was distributed. It was so embarrassing, posing while all these people from the villages were watching with looks of disgust and disapproval. And Jos shot off so many pictures; he said Brent had told him to use the whole film.

Next came a letter saying I must get a document from the police. This letter was passed to me one morning when I was about to go to the mountain with Alija. I took the letter – and my dictionary – and translated it when I reached the summer house. 'Oh my God,' I thought, 'now I have to go straight back to Zepa! I'll have to pass our house and my family will ask me where I'm going and why.'

I could think of no excuse, so I explained my problem to Alija and Fatima and we decided that the only way was not to take the road but to walk over the mountain straight down to Zepa. Fatima's brother, Halil, was staying with them and he would come with me. We set off early the next morning, with my grandfather protesting, 'You've only just got here, why are you going?' Outside it had stopped snowing but now there was frost everywhere – a white carpet on top of the snow and millions of crystals hanging from the trees. As we headed over the mountain, the air was so cold that it hurt when you breathed in, but when the sun rose everything looked so magnificent that the cold didn't matter.

Fatima was expecting a baby, and sometimes that winter I had stayed at the summer house to mind things when she had to go to the medical centre. It was my first experience of midwinter on the mountain. In the mornings you sometimes couldn't see out of the windows because they were frozen up. I would make a fire and boil water yet still the windows would stay frozen. I would breathe on the glass and for half a minute I could see out, then the ice would return. It was beautiful – you could make wonderful pictures on the window – but you couldn't see and you certainly couldn't walk outside. We had water not far away from the summer house but in winter you couldn't find it under the snow, and if you did locate it you would have to break through thick ice to reach it.

It took Halil and me five hours to reach Zepa, but at least I'd managed to avoid a family interrogation. I had a friend who was a policeman, so I found him and told him what I needed. He picked up his pen.

'So what shall I say? That you are a criminal and a thief?'

'Be serious. Just write that I am an excellent person who always behaves herself.'

'Ah, I get the idea.'

So he wrote me a reference and I put it in an envelope and dropped it off at the UN office. 'This is for you-know-who.' It felt like a huge weight off my shoulders.

The next thing Brent needed was my written permission for him to collect my passport. I had trouble translating that and had to ask Boriša, just to be sure. I wrote a letter giving the date and my name and then signed it, although it seemed to me that anyone could have written that letter and signed it to match the forged signature on the passport.

But now I would have a passport. In his letters Brent had not mentioned any real chance or possibility of my leaving Zepa, and now he was about to move to Belgrade and didn't know how easy it would be to get letters through to me from there. He wrote one last letter before he left, saying that he now had my passport, and the next thing was to arrange a date for me to go.

So still I must wait, just wait. Sometimes I was able to wait with hope, but at other times I felt angry with myself. For the first time in my life I felt helpless and it was terrible. I would think, 'All I am doing is daydreaming along with Alida, feeding myself on the romantic fairy stories of a little girl.' Before he left for Belgrade, Brent had sent more photos and now there were pictures of him all around our room: the one behind glass and another beside a little candle – everywhere photos of my darling. There was one taken in his office at Topusko, sitting at his desk in shirtsleeves, writing a report. I could see his familiar handwriting, I could see his lovely face and eyes, it was the Brent I knew. That was my favourite photo. I sat it alongside the first photo I ever had of him. Although it was already almost four months since I'd seen him there was no chance at all that I would forget what he looked like.

Before he left Zepa, Jos had assured me that the man who was replacing him as boss of the UNPROFOR team would continue to deliver and take my letters. 'He'll be just like me.'

'No one will be like you,' I said.

Jos had told Tom that no one must see the letters exchange hands, but the first time he forgot. Luckily there was only my grandmother and a couple of neighbours there to see. After that Tom was wonderful; he became my letter slave.

The letters continued to arrive from Belgrade, although not as often. In one Brent was excited: 'My darling, I have some very good news. My friend has spoken to some authorities in Sarajevo and they said that you will be permitted to leave Zepa, it is absolutely the best news I have ever received!' He said this might happen in May. But then another letter came which said he didn't know the date, but he would let me know just before.

It was spring, yet all I was doing was waiting and hoping and crying. In my country we had a saying – the only thing that happens to those who wait is that they get tired of waiting. There had to be *something* I could do. I thought about hiding myself on one of the Ukrainian trucks, but where would that get me? They could drop me off somewhere in Serbia, but then what would I do? I had no money, no passport, nowhere to go.

At home my family had begun to rebuild the house. We'd sold some sheep to buy petrol so we could cut the wood. We were helped by people who knew about building but we paid them with sheep, or some other kind of barter. The new house meant there was plenty to be done. My parents would be off cutting the wood and getting it ready while I stayed at home to cook for all the people who had come to help us. From one of those people I heard about a girl who had been taken to Sokolac, a town high on the mountain between Sarajevo and Zepa, for an appendix operation.

I thought about this. But I was known in Sokolac, so even if I somehow got to that town they would keep me there. I pushed the idea aside. But soon after, someone told me that a helicopter was due later that day to airlift all those who were seriously ill to Sarajevo. I pondered on this. The Serbs might prevent that helicopter from coming again – this could be its last trip to Zepa. If I were ill, I could be on that flight; it would be so much easier and safer than being smuggled out. I imagined how pleased Brent would be to learn that I'd got myself at least as far as Sarajevo, how much easier that would make it for him.

It was a lovely sunny morning. My father was up the road, sawing wood, my grandmother had gone to see her cousins in the next village and Alida was playing with one of her friends. So only my mother was inside.

'Right,' she said, when I got in, 'let's make some lunch.'

I went into the second room, where we kept and prepared our food, and found, on a shelf, bottles of pills that Brent had left for us. There were all kinds of pills – headache, rheumatism, stomach... I shook maybe eight tablets from two different bottles and drank them down. In my head it seemed straightforward: I would take these pills and start vomiting and the doctor would have no idea why, and wouldn't want to risk my getting worse, so he would send me off in the helicopter.

I took that first lot of pills and nothing seemed to be happening, so I took another lot – as many again, or maybe more. I drank them all down. It didn't occur to me that I might die. There was a moment when I looked at my mother and thought, 'Oh God, how can I go off and leave my family?' I started calling to Alida.

'Leave her,' said Majka, 'she's playing somewhere.'

I walked across to our neighbours' house to get something from my room and I'd just stepped back inside our place when everything went black. 'Majka, I can't see.' I collapsed on the floor. My mother fetched my father and they tried to sit me up but I was unconscious. They placed me on the truck my brother had been using to bring the wood for the house. (I don't remember any of this but they told me later.) Alida was crying; she thought I was dead. My eyes were open and my body just flopped and lay.

In their hurry, they left the door of the house wide open, and when my grandmother came home to find that empty house she thought everyone had fled. She began to pack up some things to leave, then someone told her they'd seen my parents taking me away in the truck and that I was lying on my mother's knees and hadn't looked right.

At the medical centre, the staff came and took me inside. People were gathering to look, thinking I was dead. At one point my parents thought so too, because the doctors could find no pulse. My mother began screaming and the doctors sent everyone out of the room and gave me injections. For one moment I drifted into consciousness and heard a doctor was telling me to wake up.

'You won't leave Zepa before I do,' he said. 'You can die if you want to, but you won't leave Zepa.' It was very clear; I was certain it wasn't a dream.

After that I remember nothing until I woke up lying in a bed at the medical centre. I opened my eyes and I was hallucinating: the wall beside my bed became a garden with tall fruit trees, my blanket was a cold grey stone. I realised that I could have died. They had me on a drip because I couldn't eat anything, I just threw it up again, and they'd left a needle in my arm because they'd had such trouble finding a vein. Still, I was all right. I couldn't walk, I was hallucinating, I was still in Zepa, but at least I was alive.

I hadn't gone on the helicopter – it never came – but I had, I was told, been taken in a UN vehicle with three other girls to the Serb checkpoint where permission was requested to take us to Sarajevo or Sokolac for urgent medical care. The Serbs had refused.

The day after that – my third day in hospital – a Serb shell landed beside a village school. A woman was taking her daughter to school and they'd stopped to talk to another little girl when the shell landed. The little girl was all right, but the mother and daughter were horribly wounded and two other children were killed. They brought the woman into the medical centre, to my room. There was a panic of activity and I could hear screaming and then they carried her in. She was entirely covered in blood and I could see the flesh hanging from her legs. She was screaming, screaming, screaming.

I lay in my bed watching. Someone had tried to kill this woman whom they did not even know. *I* had almost killed *myself*. It wasn't what I'd intended, and I'd had a reason for doing what I'd done, but how could I have been so stupid?

The woman's daughter was in need of treatment they couldn't provide in Zepa. Again the UN soldiers asked the Serbs to let them take this mother and daughter to a proper hospital. Again their request was refused. That little girl died. As I lay there watching her mother, a great anger built up inside me. I wanted to just get up, stand among the Serbs and shout, 'You are not people, you are animals. You can kill us – so what? What good does it do you? What is it you really want?'

Up until that moment I had thought that some day normality would return. The Serbs would say they were sorry, the terrible things they did in the name of war would be forgiven and we could again be friends. But now I thought, 'No, that can never happen. To control us this way, to play with our lives, to make people stay here and die – this is worse than war.'

After another three or four days they let me go home. Before I left, the other doctor, who was my friend, told me that he knew what I'd been trying to do. 'In your desperation to get out you almost killed yourself. I don't want to know what it was that you took. You shouldn't tell anyone. I know you want to go, but the helicopters can't be relied on. I think you'll find a better way to escape. Certainly, if anyone can do that, it is you, Aza.'

As I left I looked in at the first doctor, a man I knew but didn't like. He used to flirt with me and I never trusted him.

He said, 'What do you want?'

'I'll still get away, and you won't.'

'Over my dead body!'

At that moment I hated him. I knew he'd even be prepared to tell the Serbs if he thought I was planning to go. It made me wonder how many other people I knew felt as he did. Many of the local boys resented me because I didn't want them as boyfriends, and many of the girls disliked me because their boyfriends wanted me. Such people wouldn't like to see me escape and live the kind of life I wanted. They would have had me stay there until I died.

As a result of war, many young people were making marriages of convenience, just to help their families. A boy might be thinking, 'I know she's ugly, but her father and mother have a house that hasn't yet been burnt down, and they have a big orchard and a barrel of barley, and my family are refugees, left with nothing.' And maybe that girl, though not pretty, would be a good person and in love with the boy, and that marriage would just eat away her soul. Sometimes people didn't even pretend to like the person they were marrying; they did it just to please their families and didn't intend to remain married once the war ended.

I couldn't do that. It was their life, but it would not be mine. I would have something more – and for this they hated me. I felt that if somebody had asked all the people of Zepa, 'Should Aza go free?', ninety-nine per cent of them would have said no.

Going back home to my family made me feel so bad because of what I had done to them. I didn't want to lie but I couldn't tell them the truth. How could I say that I had wanted so badly to leave when they had always been so good to me? Every day while I was at the medical centre my mother had walked all the way to sit by my bed, and now, on my first night at home, she slept on a stretcher beside me in case I wanted water or help to go to the toilet. When I opened my eyes she would be watching me. Her concern made me feel so guilty. Alida kept kissing me and crying, she was so happy that I was alive. 'You weren't breathing,' she would tell me. 'Your heart had stopped working.'

People talked about it, of course, and some of them guessed at the truth or were told. I think quite soon most of them knew. One day, when she was angry, my grandmother told me what others had said to her. I was hugely embarrassed to think my family had heard all that and yet never said a word about it to me. That night I couldn't look my parents in the face. They might not have believed what they heard. They knew how people gossiped and that many were jealous of me. And they trusted my friend the doctor, who assured them I'd had a bad reaction to something I'd eaten.

I felt crumpled and defeated. When I set my mind on something, I was used to it working out, but now my first and only escape plan had crashed around my ears. When I told Brent about what I had almost done, he wrote back that he couldn't believe I would do such a thing.

In the weeks that followed I lived very quietly, keeping my head down. I worked harder in the house and the garden, thinking that this would prove that I had no thoughts of leaving. Sometimes I'd see my little sister watching me and read the question in her eyes: Will you leave me?

I began to see how lucky I was to be alive and to have a family who loved me so much. I think war had made me forgetful of this. I told myself, 'How could you think of leaving your family? They are the ones who really love you. Brent maybe loves you now but how long will it last? Your family might sometimes be angry at you but they will never stop loving you. A family's love goes on forever.' When I thought like this I would feel happy; I had my family and I had my girlfriends. Perhaps, at such times, if Brent had said, 'Right, it's all arranged,' I would have told him that I wasn't leaving. Certainly I began to feel indifferent about the possibility of escape. It was as if I had run out of hope.

One day I was back at the well again, doing the washing and talking to a couple of my girlfriends, when the Serbs began firing at us from across the valley. The gushing of the water in the well almost drowned out the sound of the guns, so we thought it was distant until we saw the dust rising as the bullets hit the ground close by. We ran up the road to the shelter of a barn and collapsed on the ground, where we lay, stunned by the suddenness, laughing. The shooting had stopped.

'You go home,' I told my friends.

'What about you?'

'I've got some things still to wash, and then I'll come.'

My younger friend looked worried. 'You won't take long?'

'No, and I'll be fine, don't worry.'

So off they went, and I went back to the well. There was no one else around, everyone was still hiding in their houses. I finished the washing and started to walk up the hill towards home, carrying the heavy basket. I'd almost reached the two wrecked buses at the bottom of our driveway when the firing started again. Bullets seemed to be coming at me from everywhere. I knew that I had been seen – this was a very exposed spot – and that those bullets were meant for me. I dropped the basket of washing and threw myself down beside the tyre of a truck that was parked by the buses. It was only the cab of a truck – the man who owned it lived in one of the buses and, when I went to the well, Alida had been here playing with his young daughter. But the buses now seemed to be empty so I guessed they had all taken shelter.

The bullets kept coming, smashing what windows were left in the buses and raining fragments of glass all over me. I knew the Serbs must have seen me dive behind that tyre, which, luckily, was big and very thick. After one very loud and close bang as the truck was hit, sump oil began to flow out on to my feet. I wriggled myself out of the way, I had no desire to be covered with black oil. It was almost funny. The shooting must have lasted for about fifteen minutes. Just a waste of bullets because they couldn't get me. I kept thinking, 'What if they launch a rocket? I'll be a dead woman.'

At last they stopped, but maybe they were just waiting for me to move? I stayed there for several more minutes, then began to think, 'Well, I have to leave some time, I can't stay here all night. Yes, I will go. If they start shooting again, I'll just lie down.' I knew I was taking a big risk. If they were waiting I would be an easy target. I stood up, and nothing happened, so I picked up my basket of washing and walked quickly home.

My mother was almost in tears. 'Why didn't you just forget about the washing?'

'I couldn't,' I said. 'I spent my whole morning doing this washing. Why should I let them scare me away?'

'Oh my God, Aza,' she said, 'I could kill you for this.'

'And now I'm going to hang the washing out.'

'You are not. Just come inside.'

'Majka,' I said, 'if they were going to shoot me, they would have done it as soon as I left that hiding place.' So I hung the washing out. I knew that our clothesline could be clearly seen from the Serb observation post across the valley. But I thought, 'So what? I can't hide for the rest of my life.'

When those bullets had started flying, one had just skimmed the head of Alida's friend and pierced the wall of the bus behind her. They all ran and took shelter in an old stone hut my grandfather had built. When I saw them – it would have been at least forty minutes after the shooting – the little girl who had almost been hit was still shaking and vomiting.

By then a jeep full of Ukrainian soldiers, and some

of the UNPROFOR team, had come to ask about the shooting. As a result, they erected a temporary Ukrainian checkpoint in that part of town. For two weeks they sat around with the Ukrainian flag and the UN flag flying and, not surprisingly, nothing happened. But then the Serbs did start shooting again, and the Ukrainian soldiers, poor fellows, were terrified. There they were in their helmets and bullet-proof jackets while we had no protection at all, yet they were clearly more frightened than we were. Suddenly they were under fire – the war had become real. This amused us, but we also felt sorry for them; those soldiers were so young, they were just boys.

Up until the time when I lay in the medical centre looking at that woman they had tried to kill, and whose child they had let die, there still were Serbs whom I thought of as friends. They had not hurled grenades, or burnt down homes or flown the planes that bombed us. They were sorry that those things had happened and I had thought this meant that they weren't to blame. Not any more. Now I thought, 'Those things were done by your people and so they were done for you. Being sorry makes no difference.'

One day as I stood among a crowd of people waiting for the humanitarian aid, a Ukrainian officer called out my name. He had a letter for me from a Serb man who had asked about me through a friend and he read out his name. My legs went weak. I didn't need this to happen; there were already people who thought I had connections with the Serb side. His letter asked if I was missing my Serb friends as much as they were missing me.

'Do you need any help?' he wrote. 'What can we do for you?' He wanted me to write back straight away, but they weren't my friends. Not any more.

Some of the villagers would go up to the hill across from the Serbs' lookout post and call over to them. They'd have conversations. And one day during that spring a young man I knew told me that he and four of his friends had been up there one night when the Serb soldiers had asked them, 'Where is Aza?'

'Why?' they called back. 'Why do you want to know?'

'We just want to know whether she is all right. We want Aza. If you can arrange to get Aza to us, we'll give you back your land, your villages.'

'Do you think we're stupid?' they shouted. 'As soon as you got Aza, you'd take our villages back.'

'If you get her to us, we'll give you whatever you want.'

The young men told the Serb soldiers they would have to go away and give this some thought. When he told me, I felt most uncomfortable. 'Please don't tell anyone else.' But I knew that the four others who were with him would have told their friends and soon everyone would have heard about it.

I didn't know what to make of the Serbs' request but, however I looked at it, it was disturbing. Did they imagine, after all that had happened, I could be on their side? But I was left with a nagging fear that any day the Serb soldiers might come and simply take me away.

While the new house was being built my grandmother and I had moved into the woodshed and were living there. It was an awful building but I made it as pleasant as possible, with a rack for dishes and a bench for people to sit on. The shed was made of boards that didn't fit properly together so the wind blew through the gaps. But luckily the weather at that time was good. We had a stove inside for cooking, and I did our washing outside.

That was my home when Brent's friend Robert arrived. He came with Denisa. 'This is Robert and he's from England. He's a military observer and he's Brent's friend.' Through Denisa, Robert told me that he had just come from being with Brent. 'Brent says hello.' He gave me half a kilogram of coffee beans (which made my grandmother very happy indeed) and said he had to go. I had no idea that Robert was part of Brent's plan.

This was in May, and towards the end of that month I had a letter from Brent saying that plans were now under way and I could expect to leave sometime in June – he would send me details and a definite date in his next letter.

By now our new house was taking shape and starting to look very handsome. It was large: three bedrooms and, on top of them, a big lounge, a kitchen and a bathroom, and another small room. And right at the top, like an attic, space for another two bedrooms.

I asked my father, 'Why are we building it so big?'

He said, 'Because, some winter soon, I want to live and sleep like a human being!'

There were ten men working on the house and we were feeding them breakfast, lunch and dinner. They all ate like horses, so cooking for them meant a lot of work. But now that I knew I was leaving, nothing was too hard or too much for me. 'This,' I kept thinking, 'might be the last thing I will ever do to help my family.' In whatever time was left, I was determined to do as much as I possibly could. I'd be up at half-past five in the morning and I wouldn't sit down until half-past ten at night. There was ground to prepare and seedlings to plant out, there was cooking and cleaning. I was doing the work of two or three women and that was good; I needed to keep busy and I wanted to know that, by the time I left, everything possible had been done.

Within a few days I had the next letter. It was written in Bosnian. 'I am writing you this letter in your language because it is very important for you to understand what it says. You will be leaving on Thursday 9 June. You will go with Robert. You need to be ready and waiting on the other side of Zepa, near the bridge that crosses the Zepa River at eleven a.m. and he will pick you up.' As I read this I felt my legs turn to jelly. I'd been waiting so long and now, finally, this was it.

I knew I must go. The 9th was almost a week away. Our house was nearly finished; the only thing yet to be built was the chimney, but there was no cement. In the meantime we were able to move into the basement where we had been living before. The rooms above us were virtually ready; Alida would prance around her selected bedroom. 'This is our room, mine and yours.'

'Yes, it's our room.' What else could I say?

There was so much I must do before I left. Those new rooms had to be painted and all the rugs and carpets had to be washed so they were nice and fresh on the new floors. Everything had to be moved in.

'Leave that till tomorrow,' my grandmother would say.

'No, no. I want to get it finished. I've other things to do tomorrow.'

No one thought anything of my work frenzy; it wasn't so unusual, I'd always done things at speed.

About halfway through that week Robert came with my girlfriend Demka, who had just started to work as an interpreter. She called out to me and we walked down towards the well where Robert confirmed that he would pick me up at eleven and take me to the Serb checkpoint where a man in a Volkswagen car would be waiting for me. He said everything was fine so far, and he would see me on Thursday.

From that moment I was living on adrenalin. Our very large vegetable garden was by now fully planted out – corn, tomatoes, capsicums and onions all in their separate beds – and in my last two days I hoed and weeded the whole garden. I couldn't stop, I was so full of nervous energy. I couldn't eat, I couldn't sleep, I was intensely excited. I had no doubts now, just a gnawing fear that something might happen to ruin the plan.

I tried not to let myself think about my family. I so badly wanted to say to them, 'I'm leaving. These are the last few hours we'll have together.' Most of all I wanted to tell Alida, but knew I couldn't for she would cry and that would give me away.

I had not seen my mother for almost a month, as she was staying on the mountain with my grandfather and Alija and Fatima, who was in the last stages of pregnancy. In our house there was only my grandmother, Alida, my father and me. My father had heard of someone in a village beyond the mountain who had some cement stored away for a house he hadn't built, and I was worried that he would decide I should go with him to find this man. I told my grandmother that, if he suggested this, she must say she needed me to look after her and also to milk the cow. This was quite reasonable, because living in the woodshed had taken its toll on my grandmother and she wasn't at all well. I was hoping and praying, too, that Fatima would not have her baby, because then I would be expected to go to the mountain. 'Please, please, please, Fatima, don't have the baby.' (The child was born two days after I left Zepa.) I gave my clothes away to my girlfriends. They were the only people I could tell. They knew, but I don't think they really believed it. I only half believed it myself.

On the Tuesday my father decided he would take Alida to the summer house next morning, on his way to search out the man with the cement. He thought I should go too, that it would be good for me to have a break on the mountain. My aunt, he said when I protested, could come and look after my grandmother while I was away. I knew that if I told her the truth she would give me no support. She would have me sent to jail if that's what it took to keep me there! 'I'm too busy,' I said. 'I've got so much to do.' Mercifully, he left it at that.

The next morning, when they were almost ready to leave, I looked at my sister, all dressed up in a little red jersey and red trousers, and thought, 'This is the last time I'll see her.' I started to cry. I couldn't help it; my throat clenched up and my stomach was churning. As I'd helped her dress that morning, I'd kept hugging and kissing her. She was happy to be going to the mountain. Now, when she saw my tears she said, 'Don't cry, I'll be back. I'm only staying five days with Majka and then I'll come back. If nobody comes to get me, I'll come with UNPROFOR.'

But I couldn't stop the tears that were streaming down my cheeks. 'If you want me to, I'll stay,' she said.

'No, you go. I'm just crying because I love you.'

'Okay.' She started to walk, then turned and ran back to give me a big cuddle and kiss. 'Don't cry. I'll be back.'

That made me weep all the more. I might never see her again. 'I'm not going,' I thought. 'I can't.' Then I told myself, 'You'll come back. You'll see her again.'

'What is it?' my grandmother asked. 'The way you're crying, you'd think you were never going to see her again. Shall I ask your father to let her stay?'

'No, don't. I'm just crying because I'll miss her.'

That night I packed everything I intended to take in my bag. There wasn't much – a pair of trousers, underpants, one bra and a blouse that I'd got from the Red Cross. Then I wrote long letters to each member of my family telling them that I was going. 'Majka,' I wrote, 'I know you will never forgive me for this... ' As I was writing each letter I felt that the person I loved was there with me and that I was talking to her or him. I was crying as I wrote; I felt as if my heart would explode from sorrow. But the writing was a release, and after I'd finished I felt a little calmer.

Next morning my two girlfriends had arranged to walk with me to Zepa. I was excited – and also ashamed.

'I'm just going into Zepa,' I told my grandmother.

'Will you be home by lunchtime?'

'Oh, maybe not.'

'I'll make myself lunch and leave the water on the stove so we can have coffee when you get back.'

'Fine,' I said, swallowing hard and forcing a smile. If I burst into tears again, she would definitely be suspicious.

I took my bag and left the letters on the bedside table in my bedroom. Because it was a warm day, one of my friends put my favourite black jacket over her arm and the three of us set off for Zepa. On the way my friends started to cry.

'Don't be silly,' I said, 'it's probably not even going to happen.' And I thought, 'If it doesn't, I just hope I get back before my grandmother finds those letters!'

When we reached Zepa, I saw a neighbour who was in his car and asked him if he would mind taking me, at ten to eleven, to the bridge where I was to wait for Robert. I said I had someone to visit who lived near there. He said he had nothing better to do. Because we had time to fill, we went into the office of the policeman who had written me the clearance paper. He asked me if

I had time for a coffee and I told him, no, I had an appointment.

'Then we'll have a coffee after your appointment,' he said.

'We can't,' I told him. 'I won't be here. I'm leaving at eleven o'clock.'

'You're having me on!'

'No, it's true.'

One of my girlfriends confirmed that, unfortunately, it was true, and began to cry again.

'In that case I wish you the best of luck,' he said, but I could see that he still didn't really believe us.

My two friends wanted to come with me to the bridge so without giving it a further thought I invited them to jump into my neighbour's car. By that time I was so nervous that I was shaking, but I managed to chat to the driver and decline his kind offer to come back and pick us up later. Just as he dropped us off at a corner beside the bridge, Robert drove up. I saw him look aghast at my neighbour and my two friends. 'You fool,' I thought to myself, 'you've exposed poor Robert as the UNMO who helped me to escape.' I thought for a moment that he would reverse the car and drive away, but it was too late for both of us to change our minds. I knew I had to step into the car quickly, without being seen, but I felt a surge of nausea and my knees grew weak. I thought I was going to faint.

My neighbour's mouth had fallen open. 'Where are you going?'

'Away. I'm leaving Zepa.'

His eyes grew wide. Both my girlfriends were crying. I jumped into the car, clutching my bag, my best black jacket forgotten. As the car moved off, I slumped on the seat like a rag doll, the tears welling up.

Robert handed me a piece of paper, which I couldn't

read for tears, that gave the name of the person who would meet me at the Serb checkpoint. He looked a little happier once we started moving – we had done it, we had not been seen (at least not by anyone who would cause us trouble). So far so good. But I was looking with blurry eyes at the villages we passed through, and they seemed so beautiful. *I'm going and I will never see this again.* I was thinking how much I loved this place and its people. Every good thing that ever had happened to me in my life seemed to come crowding into my head. But I reminded myself that if I stayed, I would die without ever seeing Brent again.

As we climbed up the mountain, we became caught behind a big Ukrainian truck. Robert swore and slowed down in case the driver saw in his rear-vision mirror that Robert had a civilian passenger. I would duck down at corners so I wouldn't be seen; I was glad to have something to do to stop me from thinking. Before we reached the Ukrainian checkpoint, Robert pulled over and told me to climb into the back and lie on the floor, then he covered me with blankets. At that checkpoint we were waved straight through and soon he was saying, 'Okay, you can sit up now.'

From that piece of road you could see the whole of Zepa, but I scarcely had time to look down before I had to scramble back under the blankets for the next checkpoint. Again no problems, and when I re-emerged Robert and I made a halting attempt at conversation – he couldn't speak my language and I knew very few words of English.

The last Ukrainian checkpoint was at the top of the mountain. Here we were stopped and from the back, beneath the blankets, I heard the Ukrainian soldier pressing Robert to come in for a drink. Robert was saying no, he was running late, but the other man was determined. Surely Robert could spare a couple of minutes? The soldier was even prepared to bring the drink out to the car. Robert was adamant – he really had to get going. As we finally began to move, I could hear my driver muttering about 'bloody idiots'.

Now we were in Serb territory and I was able to travel in the passenger seat once again. Robert couldn't stop grinning now that those checkpoints were behind us. Then we came to the first Serb checkpoint, and this was where I was to be collected.

There were six soldiers sitting in a hut. Robert got out and walked towards them; a short man, he seemed about half their size. I could see that they couldn't understand what Robert was telling them – that he was waiting for someone. They were all looking across at me and then one of them waved. I waved back; it seemed the wisest thing to do. Robert returned to the car. 'Everything's fine. Don't be scared.'

We sat there waiting. At one stage I saw two of the soldiers glancing our way and talking as they entered the hut. After twenty minutes a blue and white police car drove up. I felt sick, thinking that the soldiers had called the police. I couldn't go back. Please, God, not now, just when I'd got this far.

The driver and another man got out of the car. The driver was a huge man, about 35 years old, well built, dressed in Serb combat trousers and a T-shirt, with a pistol in a holster on his left side. The soldiers at the barrier stared at him; they clearly didn't know what was going on. Dragan, for that was who it was, went straight up to Robert and greeted him. They talked for a few minutes while I sat nervously in our vehicle, then Robert walked back, giving me the thumbs up as he came towards me, with Dragan following. The big man gave me a broad smile as I climbed from the car.

'Hi, my name's Dragan. You have it there on that piece of paper. I'm here to pick you up, just as you've been advised.'

I breathed again.

'Don't worry about anything,' Dragan said. 'I'll look after you as I'd look after my own child. You'll be safe, don't worry. Everything will be fine. Show me where your bags are.'

'This is my bag.'

'This one – that's all?'

'Yes, that's all.'

I gave Robert a big hug and he wished me luck. He was now going back to Zepa. No more UNPROFOR and people I knew I could trust. It was just me now, on my own now, in enemy territory.

As I walked to the car with the two men, Dragan told me they had another passenger, a soldier who was on his way home to a village a few kilometres further on. 'Just don't say anything while he's with us.' So I sat in the back with the soldier and looked out the window while Dragan and the other man chatted to each other.

After we dropped the soldier off, Dragan looked around at me. 'Now you can talk as much as you like. Don't feel you *have* to talk to us, but if you want to talk about anything at all, don't feel afraid to. We're not the war criminal kind and, definitely, neither are you.'

The three of us began to speak of what we were doing before the war. At the same time I was looking out through the windows and noticing how tranquil and normal everything appeared. All those undamaged houses, with nice white washing hanging on the line. Then we stopped to pick up a woman hitchhiker. I looked at her good clothes, her make-up, her fashionably dyed hair and I smelt her perfume. 'You bitch,' I thought. 'It's not fair!' She began to talk about herself and her job and I stayed quiet again, until we left her at Rogatica. Just a little further on, the other man left and there was only Dragan and me. He told me to come and sit in the front with him, and we began to talk.

Dragan had been to Zepa and had acquaintances there. Although he was a major in the Serb army, he didn't like what was happening in the enclave. As we drove into Sokolac, he said we would be picking up two people who would be travelling with us. They were Serbs from Sarajevo who were travelling to Belgrade. They were trustworthy, he told me, I needn't worry about what I said in front of them. Dragan produced a pair of sunglasses that he'd bought for his son. 'I think you should put these on in case you see someone you know. If you see anyone staring at you, just look away.'

We'd stopped in front of a big hotel that I knew well; its café bar used to be a popular place for me and my friends. 'Oh God,' I thought, 'any moment one of them will walk out and recognise me.' While Dragan went in to see if the couple were waiting, I sat there in dread, with my head down. Dragan returned. 'They're waiting in the café.' The couple, in their mid-twenties, were very approachable and, as Dragan had promised, easy to talk to.

The next town was Han Pijesak, where I went to high school. Because many people there knew me, I hardly dared look out. In the centre of town a policeman who had been a good friend was on road duty. He approached our car.

'That's Nikodan,' I told Dragan.

'You know him?'

Nikodan, it turned out, was also a friend of Dragan's. They greeted each other through the window, then Nikodan saw me.

'My God, is that Aza?'

'Hi,' I said.

'I can't believe it's you. Where are you going? Where did you come from?'

'I just picked her up from Zepa,' Dragan said.

'Don't lie to me. Zepa's one place nobody gets in or out of. Do you have time for coffee?'

Dragan looked at me. 'What do you think?'

'Up to you.'

So Dragan drove us back to the other end of town where there was a traditional Serb place that served good food. We bought drinks and the couple took theirs outside while Dragan, Nikodan and I found seats inside.

Nikodan was still having trouble believing his eyes. 'I thought I'd never see you again. We tried to find out where you were. I had no idea you were in Zepa.'

Just before we left, a man I knew walked in. He was one of the bus drivers who used to work with my father. I didn't acknowledge him – he was a fundamentalist type with an immense ego – but I was aware of him staring at me with disgust. Dragan noticed this too.

'He knows you?'

'Yes.'

'Okay, let's go.'

We sat outside in the car for a while and the man continued to watch me through the window. But luckily, since I was with a uniformed policeman and in a police car, there was nothing much he could say or do.

As we drove back through the town I felt more confident about looking. This was June 1994, and I had last seen Han Pijesak when I passed through in March 1992, yet it still looked the same. There were more people in the streets and every second person seemed to be wearing combat uniform, but they were still going freely about their lives.

I thought of Zepa, where, it seemed, we had been robbed of a hundred years of progress within a few months. We had been living normal lives among our families and friends in the homes we had built together, then – for some reason that we still couldn't understand – our homes and our lives had been destroyed, our freedom taken, our people killed. I looked at the streets of Han Pijesak and hated that town, hated those people. I wanted to scream, 'It's not fair,' but I watched in silence.

We crossed a river near a place where I knew – all of us in that car knew – that Muslim soldiers had tried to cross, and had been ambushed. In the battle that followed, some of our men were killed outright, others died later from their wounds. My brother and his friend were leading that group. His friend took a bullet in the chest and died. I wondered if the other three were expecting me to make some remark about the place. I didn't. I pretended I was an innocent child who had no knowledge of what had been going on.

We drove through Vlasenica, a large town whose population had been about sixty per cent Muslim. Now only Serbs lived there and you could see that many of the Muslim houses had been burnt or damaged. In the villages where both Muslims and Serbs had lived it was the same – only Serb houses would still be standing. The destruction didn't shock me in the way that seeing the streets and houses of Han Pijesak had; in Zepa, you saw destruction every day.

I had supposed that Dragan must know Brent, but now he told me that he didn't. He had been working near Sarajevo, when a request was made for someone to transport a girl out of Zepa in return for a couple of days' leave. The other soldiers, he said, had thought this meant they would have to enter Zepa and that was a risk none was prepared to take. But Dragan had reasoned that, since entering Zepa was impossible, that part of the escape must be already organised. His wife and children lived in Belgrade, and he wanted to see them, so he volunteered to go if the leave were extended to a week.

'So now,' said Dragan, 'you're getting excited. You'll be seeing your boy soon. What does he look like?' We were approaching the town of Zvornik and the bridge where Dragan now told me Brent was to meet us. 'So put on your make-up,' he said.

Only a few minutes more and it would be over! I felt so excited, then, and happy. We drove halfway across the bridge and were stopped at the checkpoint. A Serb policeman came over and asked for our ID cards. Dragan showed his card, then handed over the papers he had for me. The policeman read them.

'Won't be a moment.' He took the papers away with him.

I looked at Dragan.

'Don't worry,' he said. 'Everything'll be fine.'

Just at that moment, I looked out and saw a Han Pijesak bus belonging to the company for which my father drove. Both its driver and conductor had been close family friends. When they saw me, they jumped out of the bus and almost dragged me out through the window with their hugs and kisses. We were all laughing, but tears welled up in my eyes. A young woman joined us; she and I used to travel together on the bus when I was at university. Now she was married and pregnant. They were all asking after my family – but in a conversational way as if we all still had lives going on as usual – and about where I was going and why. I said only that I was travelling with a friend. At that point Dragan came back from the checkpoint booth and told me that we had to turn back. I managed to say goodbye to the others, then collapsed into my seat and stared blindly ahead.

'We just have to go and see someone at the police station. Your papers should have been sent here, but they haven't.'

I looked at him numbly, unable to speak.

'Don't worry,' he said. 'Don't worry, you'll be seeing Brent. If we have to, we'll swim across this river and he'll be there on the other side waiting. He must be nervous, too, just waiting. Is that him?'

I looked down the bridge and there was Brent. He was maybe fifty metres away, just propped against the side of the car, looking down. There were people all around us, but now I could see no one but Brent. Oh my God, we're this close and I have to go back! Is this going to be the last time I ever see him? Could I be so unlucky?

We drove back into the township where Dragan dropped the couple at a café and said he'd pick them up later. On the way to the police station Dragan told me he had a friend who was a senior man in the police force and he worked from an office in this town. But when we went there we found that Dragan's friend had moved to another building, so we hurried off again. Dragan walked so quickly, and I was now feeling tired and despairing. He took my arm to encourage me along. This time we found his friend and Dragan introduced us.

'This is Aza from Zepa.'

'Hi,' said the man, then he stared. *'From Zepa?'*

'Yes,' I said. 'It's a very long story.'

Dragan explained our predicament. My papers should have been sent here. His friend rang another office – did they have papers there for a Muslim girl? They didn't. He rang the headquarters in Pale and was told they had sent the papers two or three days before, so they should have arrived. Dragan's friend asked if they could send another copy. Possibly, he was told, although it could take two or three days to arrive.

Two or three days! I was appalled. How could I wait that long? I had no money, I had nothing. Dragan would look after me, I knew, but I didn't want to be looked after.

The friend was watching me. 'You know what?' he said. 'You can't be made to wait like that. I'll drive you over myself, Dragan can follow behind and when we're across you can jump back into his car and go and meet your boy.'

'Oh yes,' I said. 'Please.'

He had a new dark blue Volkswagen Golf. I sat beside him and we drove to another bridge that was really for pedestrians but was wide enough to take a car. He pulled up beside the policeman on guard and said that we were just going across for a coffee and would be back in half an hour. The guard agreed, barely glancing at me. The man beside me was his boss what else could he say or do?

That bridge was only about a kilometre from the bridge where Brent was waiting. Once we were across, Dragan's friend wished me good luck and I jumped back into Dragan's car. 'We'll be passing Brent soon,' he said. 'When you see him, tell me and I'll slow down a little and you wave to him to follow us.'

Where Brent had been waiting he could be seen from the checkpoint, so we couldn't stop there. He was still waiting, but he was looking the other way. Dragan flashed his lights and Brent looked round. As I waved, I saw his jaw drop. I thought that, in his eyes, I saw happiness, astonishment and confusion.

'He saw us?'

'Yes.'

A couple of hundred metres down the road, Dragan pulled over beside a café bar. A few minutes before I had been worrying about how I looked, telling myself Brent would want to cover me with a bag so he couldn't see me. But all those thoughts had now gone from my head. I jumped out of the car and all I felt was the happiness of seeing him.

We held each other, and we kept holding each other until Dragan came over. There were tears in his eyes.

'Oh kids,' he said, 'come on – you've got all your lives to spend together. You can separate now for a while. Let's go and have a drink.'

chapter ten

Freedom

We sat at the café and had a couple of drinks. Brent and Dragan exchanged telephone numbers, and Dragan told me to give him a call if there was anything I needed, and that we should have coffee some time while he was in Belgrade. It all felt so good. I was finally free, with a normal life to look forward to. Everything was working out, and I was happy. Oh God, I was so happy; at last we were together.

As we travelled to Belgrade with Brent and Branco, the man who'd come with him, I looked out at my surroundings. Nothing had been broken or destroyed; no grenades had fallen here. No rockets. No bullets. Although there were sanctions, this was a civilised country with barely a sign of war. Everything here was normal – except for me, but I was trying my best to appear that way.

I would see Brent looking at me in the mirror and I felt embarrassed about the way I must look. My hair was a mess and I had no make-up; it had run out long ago. It was hot and I had had plenty of cause for sweating, so my shirt was sticking to me.

But I was happy, so wildly happy that I was there, and that the deed was done. Yet a part of me was still back in Zepa. I felt as if, from the moment I received Brent's letter naming the day, something within me had been shrinking. Even walking felt odd; I could scarcely feel the ground beneath me.

I was in a continuing state of emotional turmoil. I told myself over and over that I was free, that there was nothing to be afraid of, that never again in my life would I have to face that kind of fear. But fear now seemed to be a part of me; I couldn't just clear it away like a cup from the table.

When I saw this police car flashing its lights at me, and Aza inside, I thought she'd been captured. By then we'd been waiting for nearly four hours so I was sure that something had gone wrong. But Aza was smiling and the driver was gesturing cheerfully for us to follow him so Branco and I were beside ourselves. 'We've done it! It's happened.'

On the drive back to Belgrade, Aza was in the back, and I had trouble keeping my eyes on the road and on her at the same time. I could still scarcely believe that we'd managed it all – but there she was. Back in Zepa I used to watch her in the mirror when she sat in the back of my car – a young woman trapped in a remote Muslim enclave. I had never imagined then that we would ever be together in the world outside.

I was a very happy man, driving along shouting and chattering with one eye on Aza's reflection, when I saw this policeman waving me down. He had already pulled a car over, and now he was after me. I must have been speeding, but when I saw him waving I thought, 'No, I've finally got her and there is no way she is going to be taken straight away from me again.' I put my foot down.

Branco was saying, 'Stop, you have to stop. You have to.'

'We're going,' I said.

'If he finds her in the back there'll be questions and I'm not having that. I know how difficult those Serb policemen can be.' I kept looking in the rear view mirror, and soon lost him.

We drove into Belgrade. Branco was so excited; he was such a nice man. His wife, Ljubica, was cooking a special dinner and had been expecting us back hours earlier. She was keeping watch from the balcony and, when she saw us, ran down to give us all a big hug.

Brent and I went upstairs so that I could have a shower. I needed a change of clothes, but what could I wear? The pair of trousers in my bag was crushed and dreadful. My shirt was as bad and the other shirt was just a T-shirt that had shrunk because I had washed it in water that was too hot. What I was wearing would have to do. I walked into the bathroom and locked the door and had a shower, then put all my clothes back on. Brent was in the bedroom.

'Didn't you have a shower?'

'Yes, I did.'

At dinner, I felt that everyone was watching me and worrying that after all that time in Zepa I'd be so hungry that I'd devour everything on the table. I *was* hungry, I was starving, but couldn't eat. I tried to push the food down but I couldn't swallow. Another couple, Marco and Maria, were at the dinner. Marco was a military observer from Canada, Maria was a Serb, and they were going to be married in a couple of days. Observing

Maria, seeing how comfortable she was with Marco and in this company, made me feel very small and isolated. Everyone kept watching me and asking me questions; it was as if I'd come from another planet. It felt terrible. I didn't want to be a curiosity, I wanted to be like everyone else.

But the embarrassment I'd felt at dinner was nothing at all compared with what lay ahead. That night I came to bed in my clothes, everything – even my jeans. Brent was already in bed and there I was fully dressed and excruciatingly shy.

'Are you going to sleep like that, in your clothes?'
'Yes,' I told him. 'I don't have pyjamas.'

This was such a giant leap; it suddenly seemed that we barely knew each other, and I felt foolish and inexperienced. When we made love I couldn't banish the feeling that at any moment my parents or someone would walk into the room and *catch* us.

Although I was exhausted, I couldn't sleep that night. The lights in the flat had hurt my eyes with their unfamiliar brightness, and when they were turned off there was still the glow of streetlights. So many thoughts and memories were whirling around and overflowing my head that I felt in need of a second brain to contain them all. Most were thoughts of my family. They would know by now. What were they feeling?

Brent was on leave for the next few days and we went shopping together for food and to buy clothes for me. The first thing I needed was something nice to wear to Maria's and Marco's wedding. I felt so unsure about buying clothes; the styles I had liked two years before were bound to be out of date by now, and I hadn't had time to grow comfortable with whatever was in fashion. But at least I didn't need to worry about the colours. I'd settle for black; I liked to wear black and it was always in fashion.

Down town we bought Aza a few different outfits; it reminded me of the scene in the movie *Pretty Woman*, when he takes her shopping for all those beautiful clothes. Aza would be in the dressing room trying things on and I'd be sitting in a chair, and she'd come out: 'What about this?' And I'd give my opinion. We had to fit her out from head to toe, from footwear right up to earrings.

However things might work out between us, having got Aza out, I was responsible for her. I knew that. I was her lifeline. She was a Muslim in Serb territory, and on her own there was no way she would survive.

That first week or two was a very strange time for us – a kind of total immersion therapy. We had gone from enforced physical restraint to a complete relationship, and at the same time Aza was deeply concerned about her family. Robert had been moved out of Zepa within a few days of Aza's departure, but he told me by phone that, before he left, both Aza's mother and brother had been to the Zepa HQ to ask about her. Already stories were circulating: some were claiming that she'd been killed, others were saying she'd joined up with the Serbs. Telling them the truth would have placed us all in jeopardy, but Robert had tried to reassure them. We got some Red Cross forms and Aza wrote messages to be sent off to each member of her family, but we knew that these might take weeks or even months to get through.

We communicated in her language, of which I now had a reasonable grasp, but, after all that time of struggling alone with her little dictionary, Aza now had the chance to learn and practise English. There was a video hire shop just across the road and because many of the videos were in English with sub-titles in Serbo-Croat we made good use of them.

We had to be careful about where we went and what

we did, because there was still a risk of Aza being caught. But despite that, we had fun on shopping trips, just walking around and visiting cafés and restaurants. One day, when I suggested going to McDonald's for lunch, Aza said, 'What's McDonalds?' Her question stopped me in my tracks; McDonalds was a phenomenon I simply took for granted. It was a measure of the difference between Aza's background and my own.

It was taking some time for her system to adjust to a different diet, and she was also meeting many new people – my friends in Belgrade – so the whole experience must have been overwhelming. We went to Marco and Maria's lovely wedding, although at that stage Aza was still very tired. Quite a few of Maria's Serb girlfriends were there, but Aza didn't really mix with them; I think she felt shy.

We went to dinner one night at the home of Pat Crandell, the Canadian defence attaché, who had gone out of his way to help me, and his little daughter fell instantly in love with Aza. He and his wife had been good friends to me, and Aza felt comfortable with them straight away.

At a British embassy party held on a boat there were so many people of all nationalities. The movement of the boat made me queasy so I found a seat and a Serb girl came up and started talking to me. She asked me where I came from and I told her Han Pijesak.

'I could tell you were out of place here,' she said. 'I've been watching you and when people talk to you, you don't know what they're saying. You don't understand English. So you must know somebody here.'

We talked a little more – she worked on the boat – and then Brent came over to see if I was all right.

'Is he your boyfriend?' the Serb girl asked me.

I explained that I was going with him to New Zealand.

'I don't think you need him,' she said.

'What do you mean?'

'What's so good about him? Nothing. Our boys are much better.'

'You're the only one who's said that to me. Usually girls say they envy me.'

'He might be all right, but I think you're worth more than he is, and you'd be better off with one of our boys.'

'No, I wouldn't. I like him more than I could ever like anyone else.'

She shrugged. 'Okay.'

After that I didn't want to talk to her. I said I had to go.

We took a taxi home from that party and on the way we were held up at the scene of an accident. A woman had been hit by a car as she was running across the road. As we drove past I saw her there, lying dead on the road. All I felt was irritation that she should have been so careless. Nothing else. I had seen dead people so often.

I had been to Belgrade before the war, when I lived in Sarajevo. The city hadn't changed so much, but I had. It was as if I had been asleep for two years. A long sleep, but full of terrible dreams.

On our radio in Zepa we had listened only to the news, in the hope that help was coming, or an agreement had been reached. We had to conserve the radio batteries. Now I would see things on the television that made no sense to me because I didn't know what had been happening in the world. People would talk about things of which I had no knowledge, but I'd say nothing because I didn't want to be thought stupid. So I was always trying to catch up, poring over books and magazines. In Zepa, over those two years, the only changes we saw were for the worse, but in the rest of the world change could still mean improvement, new and better ways of doing things. In Belgrade it meant dentists and doctors in private practice, and McDonalds!

In that big sleep I'd forgotten things. One of them was how to cook when you have plenty of everything: enough sugar, enough flour, enough salt. After two years of saving up these things to make something tiny, I now wasn't sure how much was enough. How much flour should I use? How much salt?

Often I felt sickened by the abundance. How could I buy those clothes, eat all that food, knowing that the people at home had so little? I was eating food I didn't even need, luxuries like chocolate, bananas, oranges, kiwifruit. I would take one bite of these things, then think how much Alida loved them, and I wouldn't be able to continue eating.

Brent and I talked to each other in Serbo-Croat, which he spoke quite well, but when I spoke quickly he couldn't understand what I'd said. He'd be shaking his head, so I'd repeat the words, sometimes over and over, which was frustrating. So, for my sake, he'd often pretend to understand.

He began to teach me a few English words each day. He was endlessly patient with me – and I, too, was patient with myself. *Unfortunately* has to be the most difficult word in the English language. I couldn't get my tongue around it, despite Brent's and Marco's coaching. Three days I spent studying that word and trying to pronounce it, and I still couldn't get it right.

We rang Dragan as we'd promised and met up with him at a hotel. He gave me a big hug and I was just as happy to see him. After our one day together it felt as if I'd known him all my life. We had lunch and he offered

Brent a lot of money to smuggle one of his relations out of Sarajevo, but Brent said, sorry, no. Dragan himself was about to return to Sarajevo, and after that day I never saw or heard from him again. *Unfortunately* I lost his phone number when I left Belgrade.

I hope some day I'll see Dragan again. He was a lovely man and I owe him so much. Though he was himself a Serb and a soldier, and was in charge of other Serb soldiers, I could never hold him responsible for the terrible things that were done.

I was constantly meeting people from various countries who knew all about me. That was unnerving. I asked Brent how they knew, and he told me that they had all, in one way or another, helped him to get me out of Zepa.

One evening, after we'd spent the day walking and shopping, and everything had been fine, I fell apart. I was a smoker then, and that night I was chain smoking. Brent watched me lighting one cigarette after another. 'Something's wrong.'

I began to cry. It was such a release – everything had been building up inside me until I felt that at any moment I would break. I wept and wept. Brent was so good, he just held me. He understood, and I saw how helpless and sad he felt, knowing that there was nothing he could do to take away my hurt.

I felt so ungrateful; for me, he had risked his life and his job. Now he must be thinking that all his efforts had only made me unhappy. I didn't ever want him to think that, because it wasn't true. I was very happy to be with him, but I missed my family. Inside me was such grief at the thought that I might never see them again and the knowledge of how much I had hurt them.

No one, not even Brent, could help me in this. What I had done could not be undone. It had been entirely my own decision, nobody had forced me to leave. Even if, in time, my family forgave me, that sense of hurt would remain inside them. I had to live with that and carry on with my life. I couldn't go back now and say, 'Oh, that was fun. I did some shopping and now here I am.' I loved them and missed them terribly, but I didn't want to return.

The following week Brent went back to work and Branco and his wife Ljubica went to the Krajina to see Branco's father, who was ill. I was left on my own in the flat, not knowing how to occupy myself. There was little I could do in the way of housework because Ljubica did all that before she left. I would go out on the balcony, come back in, lie down, get up, go out on the balcony...

It was risky for me to go into town. The sanctions were very strict and the police could stop you on any pretext. If they questioned me I could claim to be Serb but they would then want documentation. Nevertheless, one day I walked to the market and spent a long time looking around the stalls, just for the pleasure of being in an open space. But all the time I was a little anxious.

With Brent, no matter where we went, I felt completely safe. As long as I was with him no harm could be done to me – it wasn't entirely logical, but it was how I felt.

A few days after I'd returned to work Sanela rang from Sarajevo. As soon as she spoke I knew something was wrong. 'What's happened?'

'I can't tell you,' she said, 'but Julian will be in touch.'

'Sanela, what's going on?'

She just repeated, in a strained voice, 'Julian will talk to you about everything.'

I'd been found out! I could feel my heart pounding.

The call came from Julian. 'The CMO knows that Aza has left. He knows that you were involved, and Robert too. He's interviewed Robert and you can expect to be in trouble on this one.'

'Yes,' I said. 'I know that, mate.' The chief military observer was a Dutch general who was not at all well regarded by the observers.

'Chances are he'll have you summonsed to Zagreb for a meeting. Just remember I'm here for you. I'll do everything I can to help you out.'

'I appreciate that. Thanks very much.'

And I did appreciate it. It was very good of Julian. I knew that, by calling, he was giving me the chance to prepare myself mentally, but instead I panicked. I knew that I could be repatriated, and would probably be in big trouble when I returned to New Zealand. I had got Aza as far as Serbia, but I didn't know how I was going to manage the next step. Despite the likelihood of being found out, I had been gambling on serving out those last two months of my mission, and having that time to organise a way of getting Aza out of Serbia.

Later that day I got a call from Lieutenant-Colonel John Garnett, New Zealand's senior national observer and the point of contact for all the New Zealand UNMOs. The highest-ranking officer from each country had the position of senior national observer and they were all answerable to the CMO. He said that he needed to see me and talk about my recent activities. The CMO also wanted to see me; he was not very pleased with my behaviour.

Both John Garnett and the CMO were in Zagreb, so I drove down there – it was a Thursday – and faced up to the CMO. It was a very short interview.

'So what have you got to say for yourself?'

'Well, sir, at the end of the day I've saved a life. It's as simple as that.'

He wanted to know how much I had paid and whether I'd exchanged any military secrets. I could tell he was just guessing. Then he tried to tell me that the Bosnian Serbs were unhappy about what I'd done.

'The Bosnian Serbs knew all about it,' I replied. 'They're just trying to get some mileage out of this by accusing the UN of acting outside their official capacity.'

The decision on my punishment, he implied, was out of his hands; the matter would have to be passed on to New York. In fact I later discovered that he simply asked New York to approve an order that I be repatriated. After my four-hour drive from Belgrade, the interview was over in about ten minutes.

I then went to see John Garnett, from whom I was expecting severe discipline, but he was very good to me. We had lunch together and I told him as much of the story as I felt I could, explaining that Sergey had organised it, made it possible. He warned me that the system wouldn't look kindly on what I'd done: mixing my personal life and my professional duties, showing partiality. I said that I accepted that; if I were to be repatriated, so be it.

Back in Belgrade I worked out that, since it was almost the weekend and the New York headquarters would be closed down, the decision about what to do with me wouldn't be made for a few more days. Assuming that I would be repatriated, I must use that time to get Aza out, or she could be left in Serbia while I was being shipped off back to New Zealand. With only a Bosnian passport Aza should never have been in Serbia, so how would she get through their border controls without being arrested?

Branco had a contact on the Serbo-Hungarian border; I had been relying on that, but now Branco and Ljubica were away and I didn't know how to contact them. How else could we arrange it? I was at my wits' end trying to think of schemes and contacts. We tried Dragan, but he'd gone back to Sarajevo.

Clutching at straws, I went to one of the embassies to talk to someone I knew slightly. He in turn put me on to someone else who 'might be able to help'. I went to see this man, without knowing who he was, what he did or why he did it, and that visit turned out to be both an eye-opener and a godsend. When I told him our story, he turned up his stereo and said he believed he could help us. The Serb government was indebted to him over a recent bending of the immigration rules for a military VIP, and that would help him greatly in taking care of our problem.

While I was there he made some phone calls, then told me he would ring me in a couple of days, by which time he should have things worked out. Quite clearly he was used to this kind of subterfuge; he told me he was 'well known' and he suspected his phones were tapped and his rooms bugged. My impression was that he had infinite experience of 'ironing out' the difficulties of illegal exits and entries all over the world. Under the circumstances, I found that reassuring.

I left feeling hopeful but telling myself that I still needed to plan for the worst outcome. If I were sent to New Zealand while Aza was still stranded in Serbia, I would need to come back and get her. That would require a visa, so I visited a local government agency that issued Serb visas for the military observers. I told someone I knew there that I needed a visa for myself, covering at least the next three months. No problem, he said.

Tucked away in a dingy part of town I found the Hungarian embassy and showed them my passport and Aza's. Did hers require a visa? No, but mine did, as I already knew. I filled out the application and they said my visa would be ready later that afternoon. I rushed off to see a contact I had at the British embassy to organise a British visa and make sure Aza's would be stamped without questions. But by the time I'd done that and returned to the Hungarian embassy, it was closed for the weekend. 'Oh no,' I thought, 'my passport's in there!' What if I were called back to Zagreb to be shipped off home before the embassy opened on Monday? How would I explain the lack of my passport to the UN authorities?

We made it through that weekend without my needing the passport. On the Sunday the man on whom we were pinning our hopes rang and told me that everything was arranged: we were expected at the Hogosh border crossing. So I rang a hotel in Budapest and booked Aza a room, then told my boss I needed some time off next day and would he cover for me? Then I studied a map to be sure I knew the route and the terrain through which we had to travel. On Monday I raced to the Hungarian embassy, arriving just as they opened, to pick up my passport and visa. Then I returned to the flat to collect Aza.

For five days I'd been rushing around trying to get everything organised, and we were about to find out whether I'd succeeded. I kept telling myself that, having got this far, and been through so much, we could manage anything. We'd already achieved the unachievable, so what was there to worry about?

All the same, we were both on edge. Ever since that weekend in Sarajevo I'd been running on adrenalin, a continuous version of the occasional adrenalin rushes I'd experienced as a pilot. I knew that the pressure was getting the better of me, that I was approaching the point of complete exhaustion.

It was a horribly hot day and we had a two-and-a-half- to three-hour drive to the border. The route was through country I'd never seen before, so I didn't know if we could expect to come across military activity, checkpoints or police. Or what difficulties these might cause us. On top of all that, against the rules, I was taking a UN car out of a mission area.

Aza, naturally, was feeling very anxious. I was aware of her looking around at this country that had been Yugoslavia, her homeland. I knew she was thinking that she might never see it again. We stopped somewhere for lunch, then pushed on. When we reached the border, there were two places of entry and I didn't know which to choose. Which guard looked the most likely? Then I decided that both should know we were coming, so we lined up in a queue and waited. Our turn came and I handed over our passports. The guard just glanced at mine, which was on top, and then saw Aza's.

'Just a moment, please.' He went inside.

Here we go, I thought.

He came back out. 'How many sheep are there in New Zealand?'

'Ah, sixty million,' I guessed.

He gave a bit of a grin and my heart dropped back into place. He handed back our passports. 'Good luck.'

He waved us through to the Hungarian border guard. We weren't expecting any difficulty on that side, but the guard was clearly suspicious. He stood shaking his head while he pushed Aza's passport under the ultraviolet light again and again, and we waited in dread. It was a legal Bosnian passport; he must have been trying to figure out how its owner could have got past Serb border guards. Finally he just shrugged, handed it back and waved us on. We were in Hungary, and Aza was now a free citizen!

I was anxious to return to Belgrade before my absence became a matter of interest. It took about half an hour to reach a town and, after a fruitless search for the railway station, we had to find someone who could speak English in order to get directions. The next train to Budapest was due in soon, but the woman at the ticket office wouldn't take American money so we had to scramble back into the car and rush down town to find a bank. It was around four o'clock and I was afraid they might be closed, but we found one, exchanged the money, drove back and bought the ticket. Giving Aza a fistful of money, I saw her on to the train, telling her to take a taxi from Budapest station to the hotel. 'Then wait for me, okay?'

Once I had reached Hungary, Brent had told me, I'd be just like anybody else. No one could take me and put me in prison, or make me go back to Bosnia. He didn't know how long it would be before he could join me in Budapest, but whatever they had in store for him at least he would know that I was safe. I didn't want to leave him. I was worried about how I would manage, alone and not speaking the language. But of course I would go. I would do whatever he said. I had absolute trust in him. If he'd told me I must go and live in Japan for a couple of months, I would have gone.

Already we were more at ease with each other. The longer I knew him, the better I understood just how much he had done for me, and the more I appreciated his kindness and understanding. I think that getting me out of Zepa had proved the easy part – the hard part was living with me, for in Belgrade I'd been a different person from the Aza he'd known. I'd been so bound up in guilt and conflict. My feelings were so confused. It must have been hard for him to know, when I was so unpredictable and emotionally unstable, what to do or say. The smallest thing could upset me. Yet throughout that time he was always gentle and caring. I will never forget that. His shoulder was always there for me.

All the way, on that trip to the border, I tried to be calm and quiet as a mouse. I didn't want him to think I was worried; he already had enough problems.

At the railway station in the town of Szeged we said goodbye and he gave me money; $500 in American currency – and there seemed to be so much of it. It was terribly hot inside the train. I found an empty carriage and sat there, but people got on at other stations and all of them seemed to be speaking different languages. I sat watching them, feeling hot and scared. How would I know where to get out? As the train pulled in at a station I looked at a woman sitting nearby. 'Budapest?'

'No, no, no.' She managed to convey to me that she was going to Budapest. Good. I only had to follow her.

When she stood up to leave the train, I grabbed my bags – thanks to all our shopping in Belgrade I was no longer travelling light – and we stepped down on to a platform crowded with people. I clutched my bags tightly and tried to stroll so that potential criminals wouldn't guess that I was lost and alone. I didn't have a clue where I should head, then I heard someone calling, 'Taxi', so I set off in that direction.

When I gave the taxi driver the name of the hotel that Brent had booked me into, he asked me a question and I had to tell him that I didn't understand. I thought he would take advantage of my being a foreigner, so all the way I was taking note of the streets we passed through in case we drove down the same one twice. I thought that would also help give me some sense of my surroundings once I'd reached the hotel.

It was a large hotel, and when the taxi left I stared at all those doors wondering how I would find the reception desk. The first door I tried turned out to be the right one. A receptionist gave me a key and took me upstairs, while a porter trotted behind with my bags, and all the time she was talking away to me in Hungarian. She showed me my room and, when she'd gone, I jumped on the bed; yes, yes, yes! I was wildly happy. I'd made it! I was safe, I was free and I had a bed to sleep in. I'd been there barely half an hour when Brent rang. I was pleased that I could sound happy and excited, so this time he wouldn't have to think, 'Oh God, she's upset again!'

I drove back to Belgrade feeling tired and stressed. The interminable toll gates, where they charged you so much to travel a hundred kilometres of road, seemed like the last straw. I got home, rang Aza, then collapsed into bed.

The next day I received a call at work. 'Be in Zagreb this afternoon. You are leaving the mission area in a few days.' I thought, 'Thank God she's gone. We were just in the nick of time.'

Back at my flat, I packed up all my gear, left a note for Branco and Ljubica and then drove to Zagreb to begin the complicated UN checkout procedure. My biggest worry at this point was my actual travel arrangements. These were done by the UN and the stopovers were a matter of luck. I could be booked back to New Zealand via Zurich, via London, via Hungary, via anywhere.

No good, I thought. Whatever happens, I somehow have to get back to Budapest. I also wanted a week or two in London, which would give me time to sort out Aza's New Zealand visa. When I asked for this, I was told that the matter of my return was now in New Zealand's hands, so a fax requesting some leave time in London was sent off, through the official UN channels, to New Zealand.

I tried to get hold of the UN travel clerk to find out

what the arrangements might be, but she was a busy woman and hard to track down. So I began to go through the signing-off process, after which I still had to sort out my gear and decide what I could take with me and what needed to be packed up and couriered home. Then I received my reply concerning London in a fax from Land Force Command at Takapuna. It said leave in London was denied and I must come straight home. 'To face the music,' I thought ominously. I mulled this over but decided that, whatever happened, I wasn't going home without Aza.

The New Zealand army had told me to fax them my travel arrangements, but I didn't yet know what these were. Finally, I saw the UN travel clerk and asked if my travel had been arranged. She went searching through the paperwork. 'Something's not right here.'

'What do you mean?'

'You're not supposed to be going for another month and a half.'

'I'm being repatriated.'

'Oh. Well, in that case we've got nothing to do with your travel. You'll have to organise it yourself.'

I drafted a fax to New Zealand – 'UN unable to organise my travel and am having to do it myself. Will be back in New Zealand asap. Will advise.' I completed the signing-out procedure, then rang to find out when the next train was leaving for Hungary.

I had been in the hotel for about five days, and Brent had rung me each morning and evening. Now he called to say that he was on his way and would be arriving that night about ten or eleven o'clock. It was only a few hours to wait, but it seemed like two or three days. I tried to sleep to make the time pass, I counted up to thousands, but I was still wide awake with excitement.

At the hotel everything and every day had been wonderful. On that first morning after finding the word for it in my dictionary I had gone to breakfast. I took my dictionary with me and just followed everyone else. Breakfast was self-service so I didn't have to face a menu I couldn't understand. I wanted to go out so I selected an old couple who, from the way they were dressed, clearly weren't going back to their room, and I followed them. It worked perfectly. They walked around town and I walked around town and got my bearings. All around me people were talking but I couldn't understand a word they said. That was all right, though, unless I got lost and needed to ask directions.

At lunchtime I couldn't go and order food, and I couldn't find a bakery, so I went to a supermarket and chose things off the shelf. I took the food back to eat in my room. Each day I'd grown a little more confident. I would walk further and even shopped for some clothes, but only when a shop wasn't busy because it took so long for me to explain what I wanted.

Around eleven o'clock that night I heard the knock on the door that I was waiting for. The porter was with him, carrying bags. My God, I was happy. I felt as if I'd been reborn. We spent the next two days together in Budapest, and they were the happiest I had known. Everything was perfect.

I'd been trying to get us on a flight to London but they were all fully booked. Then I learned that there might be a chance of getting seats out on the Sunday if we queued for stand-by, so we arrived early and lined up. By the time our turn came, there were only a couple of first-class tickets available. I booked them up on my Visa card, and we were on the first step of our journey home.

I had only been able to organise a British entry visa

for Aza, so when we landed we had trouble with the customs officer at Heathrow. She was nice about it, but without an exit visa Aza could have stayed in the country as long as she liked as an illegal immigrant. I explained that we were to arrange her visa for New Zealand and then we'd be leaving Britain. I pleaded with her, and finally she let us through.

Aza was feeling ill. She had gone through so much change in such a short time, not only a radical change of diet, but huge environmental and psychological changes. For two and half years she had lived an almost stone-age existence, and now it was jet travel, foreign languages, cities bursting with people. We took a bus to the hotel, and as soon as we reached our room she ran to the toilet and began vomiting. She was running a temperature and feeling ill and exhausted.

Before we collapsed, I rang my parents because I knew they'd be worried. I'd phoned them from Belgrade to tell them we'd got Aza out, and then later from Zagreb to say I was in a bit of trouble and might be home earlier than expected. They were sympathetic about the whole situation as, naturally, I'd talked to them about Aza in March when I was home on leave. Now I asked them to ring the Land Force Command and explain that I was stuck in London trying to organise a flight home. Since I was already in trouble, I was at least going to wait until the New Zealand High Commission opened in the morning, and I was entitled to a stopover en route to New Zealand.

After a good night's sleep we woke early and visited Indira, who had just moved from Zagreb to London. It was so good to see her; she had been such a help to me in organising Aza's passport. From there we went straight to New Zealand House to see a woman who knew about our situation; I'd spoken to her a couple of times, and Colonel Pat Crandell had seen her too. I was counting on her being there, so when I saw a sign saying that the visa office was open only in the afternoons, I charged on in regardless. The woman we needed to see was there, knew who we were and was willing to talk to us immediately. She interviewed us, made some notes, went away to stamp Aza's passport and wished us luck.

Thomas Cook, just across the street from New Zealand House, told us there was a flight leaving for New Zealand that afternoon. I calculated we would just have time to get back to our hotel, pack up our bags and make it to Heathrow. From the hotel I made another call home: 'This is our flight. Can you ring Land Force Command and tell them my arrival time in Auckland?' We made it to the airport in time and fell into our seats. We were travelling via Bangkok and Perth, a twenty-four-hour journey. I didn't sleep in all that time. I couldn't. I was exhausted but worries kept churning in my head. Could Aza be happy without her family and in a land so different and so far away? How much trouble was I in? Had I brought disgrace to the New Zealand armed services? What if I lost my job?

Whatever happened, I tried to tell myself, I'd just have to take it in my stride.

When we left Hungary on the plane to England I had watched out the window, thinking that every second was taking me further away from my family. I was going home, I told myself, home to a place I'd never seen. And, like it or not, I would have to live there.

It was such a long, long flight from London. We landed in Auckland early in the morning. It wasn't yet light so I couldn't see anything, but I was happy to be on the ground again. A man from the army was there to meet us. Brent said I should wait at the airport while they went to get the car. Outside the sky was growing light but it was overcast.

As we drove through farmland, I felt as though I were on some tropical island, there were so many bushes and trees that were unfamiliar to me. The wild flowers growing beside the road were so beautiful that at first I thought they were part of somebody's garden. Everything looked very clean and tidy and washed by the rain. The toetoe was out; I'd never seen such a plant before. I saw how the flax bushes had been whipped and battered by the wind, which wasn't a promising sign. The roads were full of Japanese cars, which impressed me, because at home such vehicles were rare and very expensive. Also, most of these cars were new.

We reached our destination and got out of the car. It was cold and I was shivering, not just from cold but also from fatigue. All I wanted to do was sleep.

As soon as we were through customs I was taken to see the brigadier at Land Force Command, since technically I was still working for the army. He sat me down and said he had Lieutenant-Colonel Garnett's report. Repatriation was not done lightly, and the army was displeased with me, but I was now back in the employ of the air force, who had been informed of the situation; any disciplinary action was up to them.

That afternoon I went off to see the air commodore, expecting the worst. I'd be told that I had brought disgrace to the New Zealand defence forces; they'd probably toss me out. But when I reached the commodore's office, it wasn't an irate man who greeted me.

'Welcome back,' he said, and he shook my hand. He said a red line had been drawn beneath the past and it was now forgotten. So what would I like to do next? Did I still want to do the flying instructor's course?

Relief flooded through me. What I wanted at that point was to sleep for a long, long time. I asked for three months' holiday. He agreed and sent me off to one of the administration officers so that the leave could be arranged. After the holiday I would begin my flying instructor's course.

The air force was letting me put it all behind me and get on with my life. It was a huge weight lifted from me. After all Aza and I had been through, being branded a disgrace and losing my job would have destroyed me. Why had I been treated with such leniency? I had no idea. Had the air force understood my situation and felt some sympathy? Or had something gone on behind the scenes? Had someone, perhaps my friend the Canadian defence attaché, somehow pleaded my case at an official level? To this day I still don't know.

Because I was so cold – it was the middle of winter – Brent said I should have a coat, so we went shopping and bought a beautiful full-length creamy one. Then we were given a free lipstick to match the coat and went looking for boots. But all we could find were the kind you'd wear when riding a motorbike, so we went back to the motel. While I had a sleep, Brent went off to see another one of his bosses, and when he got back he was very, very happy. Next morning we had breakfast at a restaurant down by the sea, a novelty for me. It was exciting; there was excellent food and a tree covered with lemons. Brent asked if I wanted us to stay in Auckland for a few days, but I said, no, I wanted to be finished with flying.

When I saw Christchurch from the plane window, it didn't look like the photos in the book Brent had showed me that night of the chicken dinner. As we walked along the corridors of the airport my legs were quaking; I was about to meet his family. This must be them – his mother, Avis, in trousers, with hair cut short like a boy's, and his sister Leanne. Yes, they looked nice.

They were very happy to see Brent, and full of questions for me, which Brent answered on my behalf. As we drove home, I looked out at the houses with some dismay. They seemed so frail and temporary. Our houses were built of concrete and, to me, these wooden structures looked more like woodsheds. When we got to the Kings' house my worries seemed at first to be confirmed; Brent's parents were renovating, and downstairs was in work-in-progress chaos. But the work on our bedroom had been finished – the carpet had only just been laid when Brent's mother and sister left to meet us – and it looked new and nice with a big bed and the smell of fresh paint.

As we walked through the house I was trying to walk very carefully in case I stumbled or knocked something over and Brent's mother and sister would think I was hopeless. I was trying so hard to seem natural and normal. Upstairs we all had coffee – instant coffee and not at all like ours, but I was getting used to it. They were talking and asking me questions, and I would look at Brent to interpret what they said and then to interpret my reply.

The chair I'd sat down on was like no other chair I'd sat on in my whole life. Brent told me it was a La-z-boy and that I could pull the lever and raise the leg rest, so I pulled and the leg rest shot up. When it stopped, it was much too high to be comfortable. *Oh God, I've done it wrong! Why did I even touch the lever?* When they asked if it was too high, I said no, no, pretending that sitting with my legs above my head was just what I wanted. It was so embarrassing. I could see them looking at me and thinking how uncomfortable I must be.

After a while I needed to go to the toilet and had to work out how I could get out of that chair. Finally I slid off it sideways. Later Brent demonstrated how to use the lever, but it wasn't until one day when I was in the house alone that I dared to get back into the chair and try it out.

From the moment I met Brent's mother and sister I liked them very much, but I was still worrying about meeting his father, and as dinnertime approached and he was due to arrive home, I felt increasingly nervous. But when the time came, it was fine. Colin gave me a kiss and we looked each other in the eye. I thought, 'I don't know what you're thinking, but I'm thinking that you're all right.'

At dinner I watched everyone else and did just what they did. There was meat and many different vegetables. I watched to see in what order they should be eaten, but everyone did it differently so I decided the order didn't matter. There was pumpkin, which I thought at first was just for decoration. Never before had I eaten pumpkin as a vegetable. At home we fed pumpkins to our animals and when, during the war, we ate it ourselves, it was ground up and made into bread. I tried the pumpkin and it was delicious.

Brent said it was acceptable for me to leave food on my plate, but there was nothing I didn't want to eat. I was hungry and everything tasted wonderful.

The next day it was all a little easier. When I looked out our bedroom window I saw a swimming pool. I imagined us making a swimming pool back in Purtići – how long it would take us to dig and to build the wall. Beside the pool was a palm tree and, even though this was winter, Christchurch still felt warm to me.

That second day all the aunts and uncles and cousins came to meet me. I felt as if I were under a microscope, with everyone taking turns to study me. At one point I asked Brent if I could have a glass of water. 'Just go into the kitchen,' he said, 'and help yourself.'

I was shocked. I couldn't possibly do that. In my country that would be such bad manners! At that stage I was still a stranger, not part of the family. 'Your mother will ask me what I'm doing there. What if I knocked something over or broke something? Please get it for me?'

One day, at lunch, we had pikelets. I watched people spreading theirs with butter and jam, but I didn't feel like something sweet, so I asked Brent could I put salt on mine. 'If you want to.'

I reached for the salt and suddenly saw that everyone had stopped eating and was watching me. I pretended not to notice. It was *my* pikelet. I spread on a little butter and sprinkled it with salt.

Once I was home relief flooded through me. Everything was all right. I had Aza and I still had my job; my life was falling back into place. The emotional rollercoaster of love, anger, frustration and fear that I'd been riding for the last ten months now just fell away and I slept and slept and slept. Day in, day out for two months I would sleep for twelve- or fourteen-hour stretches.

Some of the men, when they came back from Bosnia, suffered stress and anger problems because of what they'd seen and experienced. In the mission areas we'd hear stories about observers behaving oddly when they returned home. Some would go around the whole house turning on all the lights and electrical gadgets just for the delight of having a power supply. There was one who, reportedly, went home and filled up buckets and buckets of water. When his mother asked him what he was doing, he told her it was their emergency supply in case the water was disconnected.

When I had finally slept off my exhaustion, I felt just fine, but I knew that those ten months had changed me. Mostly they'd shaken up my priorities – no more would I complain over little disappointments or inconveniences. Remembering Zepa, how could I?

We went on holiday, driving to the southern lakes and up into the mountains. The South Island was very beautiful. I was amazed by the treeless hills and mountains, which looked slightly absurd, like a man caught naked. And I looked at the smooth, wide roads and thought of Zepa's rocky and mountainous tracks.

In Wanaka we stayed with Nermina, whom we'd met on the plane coming to Christchurch. She, too, had come from Bosnia to be with a Kiwi air force pilot – Robbie Nicholls, one of New Zealand's first UNMOs in Yugoslavia. This was good for me; Nermina felt like a piece of home. But she had been in New Zealand for five months and could speak the language. There was a whole crowd of people all staying at the same place and everyone spoke English except me. I was constantly aware of missing out on the conversation.

From Wanaka Brent and I went on to Queenstown. There we were on our own again and it was restful; in fact, it was just perfect. Even there, though, there were moments when I would suddenly feel a great loneliness, and know that there was a part of my heart even Brent couldn't fill. That part belonged to Alida, and it ached for her.

It was September when we went to the North Island and drove up just past Ohakea to Bulls, where we would live. We moved into our little house and for the first few days everything was fine. Then, one day, I went for a walk with my neighbour, Leisa, and her two little boys, and I was talking to the children in my improving English when four jet planes came over, flying low. By the time we heard them they were almost above us. I knew that moment too well; it was when you knew there was nothing you could do.

My instinct was to throw myself on the ground, but I couldn't even do that. Memories came flooding back and I stood there paralysed with fear. I saw Leisa's expression jump from laughter to shock as she looked at me; she knew enough about my past to understand what was happening. I was trembling, I felt sick.

'Oh, no,' breathed Leisa. 'I'm sorry. Are you all right?'

After that I didn't go outside very often and when I heard the planes coming I would turn up the TV to try and drown them out. But sometimes at night when Brent was at work I'd hear planes, probably Skyhawks, but they'd sound to me like big aircraft flying up high, and I would be waiting, waiting for the change of sound as they dived to drop their bombs.

When we'd been in our little house for about six months I was pegging out the washing when a jet came low overhead. Without thinking, I dropped the washing and ran towards the kitchen. Before I got there I stopped myself: 'Why are you running?' I almost laughed at myself, but then I went into the living room and cried.

I think it will always be like that for me. Sometimes I am fine, and I think the memories will go and leave me alone, but then they return. You can't shut them out. You can't run away from them. You can only try to lay down good memories on top of the bad ones.

Epilogue

For the rest of the year I wrote letter after letter to my family, not knowing if they would ever arrive, always hoping for a reply. But nothing came and the silence was a hard thing to live with. I felt that my heart had been split in two; half of it was in New Zealand with Brent but the other half was still in Zepa with my family.

I knew only too well how they'd be feeling. They would be angry at me for deceiving them, and beneath the anger would be a great sadness. Not all of them would be angry; Alida wouldn't be angry, and neither would my mother, but their sorrow would be the deepest of all. All those small-minded people who had disapproved of me so fiercely would be having a marvellous time making up stories. I needed my letters to reach my family to counteract that poison.

Christmas came and Brent and I went down to Christchurch to spend it with his family. While we were there, just before Christmas Day, the Red Cross delivered a message from my family. It said they were all fine and had received two of my letters, both on the same day. That was the best Christmas present I could possibly have had. My other letters must have gone missing, but at least now we were in contact. I was so relieved and happy, and Brent's family were glad for me. I shall always feel grateful to the Red Cross. I don't how many people appreciate the work that they do, but to my mind they are a wonderful organisation.

In February Brent decided that we ought to get married. I was staying in Christchurch with his parents and he was in Ohakea working. He must have missed me; one night he went drinking with a good friend, Shane Harrison – Whitey, and at two o'clock in the morning Whitey, who was drunk, tried to ring me about Brent's big decision. Avis answered and said I was asleep, so he told her the news. I learned about my engagement thirdhand.

We decided we'd get married in March at Ohakea. Brent's mother was excited about the wedding and began making plans. It wasn't a big wedding. The ceremony was held at the base commander's house, and Brent's family came up and we had our friends from Ohakea. Brent's sister, Leanne, and our Bosnian friend Nermina were my bridesmaids and there were two little flowergirls. Brent's father gave me away. We said half our vows in English and the other half in Bosnian, and Julian Tangaere did a reading. Julian, who had been to Zepa and had met my family, was one of the people who had helped to make our marriage possible. It was good to have him there.

Everyone was trying to make it feel comfortable for me, but still I was nervous. I couldn't follow the speeches or understand the telegrams; everyone would laugh and I wouldn't know why. I looked around at the faces of all those very recent friends and longed for the reassurance of an old friend's glance.

We ceremonially opened and drank the bottle of *rakija* that Kušic' had presented to Brent at Lukavica after he had fulfilled his part of the bargain that set me free. The wedding was filmed on video, then Brent, Nermina and I recorded a special videotape in Bosnian to send to my family, along with the wedding video. We didn't just talk about the wedding, we talked about everything. I told Alida how much I missed her. She mustn't feel upset when she saw those two little flower-girls, I said, she was still first in my heart. It should have been her walking behind me.

I'd had a letter from Amira, my girlfriend in Zepa. She told me how, in the first months after I'd gone, Alida used to come to her place to play with her little sister. And she'd say that she'd been waiting and waiting for a letter from me but nothing had come and I didn't love her any more. Then she'd burst into tears and run away.

In July 1995, the Red Cross delivered two more messages from Bosnia. One was from the Mehmedovic family, the other from Aza's girlfriend Amira, who was now living in Srebrenica. Both reported that everything was fine, but we saw by the dates that both messages had been sent over two months before. At that time, we learned later, the Serbs were not allowing either the humanitarian aid vehicles or the Red Cross to enter Zepa.

Aza replied to both messages immediately. Despite her worry, anger and sense of helplessness over her family's situation, she was now making good progress in her recovery from the trauma of war. The graphic nightmares she used to have almost every night now haunted her only about twice a week.

But then, only a few days after those messages of reassurance, the Serbs invaded Srebrenica.

We learned of this as we sat in our home watching

the television news. The ramifications were obvious and horrifying. Even against impossible odds, there was no way that the Bosnians would surrender without a fight. Aza's brother, Alija, and her father, Mustafa, were frontline soldiers and might be already in the battle. Even worse, Zepa was the township closest to Srebrenica. If Srebrenica – another designated 'safe area' – were taken, it was inevitable that Zepa would be the next to fall. The enclave was under-resourced in both soldiers and weapons; five times during the early stages of war the Zepa militia had fought off the Serbs, but now it was clear that General Mladic had amassed considerable troops and hardware around Srebrenica and would steamroll his way through the eastern Bosnian enclaves.

As we all now know, Srebrenica was taken with brutal ease. On TV we watched hysterical women whose horrified testaments were often translated incorrectly by the media interpreters, but Aza heard all too clearly what they were saying. As the tales of Nazi-style executions and atrocities emerged, her distress rocketed. I tried to shelter her as much as I could from the newspaper and television reports. I clung to the remote hope that the United Nations or NATO would intervene, at least in time to save Zepa.

When we saw the Serb soldiers moving into Srebrenica I was stunned. How could they be allowed to invade a safe area? Was the word 'safe' merely a joke that meant nothing? Was UNPROFOR just there to listen to the Serb generals and let them do whatever they wanted? Until that day I had listened to any news reports on Bosnia in the constant hope that things were improving, and that one day soon we might be told that the war was over and everyone was free to lead a normal life again. That appalling offensive on Srebenica went on for ten days, a horror story that all the world was watching. Now everyone could see for themselves the truth of what we had been telling them. The world had waited and done nothing, and now the world was watching and doing nothing.

I was angry. I was sad. I was distraught. When the reports came of men being bulldozed into mass graves and I heard news commentators voicing disbelief, I thought, 'Just wait until those husbands and brothers and fathers fail to come home and their women go searching and find their men are not in prison, not in hiding, not anywhere.'

After Srebrenica, the Serbs took a little break, presumably while they reassembled their troops and artillery around the pocket of Zepa. Because of the topography and because it was already surrounded by Serb territory, taking Zepa presented no challenge. The presence of the UNPROFOR Ukrainian company would prove to be no deterrent.

The bullets, grenades and rockets started to fly early in the morning. The Ukrainian battalion began to pull out – those soldiers were in as much danger as anyone else. On TV we saw Mladic saying that the Serbs wanted all the people of Zepa to leave peacefully. They would transport the women and children out of the enclave and the men should surrender and be taken as prisoners. But who could believe him?

When we heard that Zepa had fallen Aza began to cry and wail, and for three days she wept almost constantly. She was inconsolable. When the TV news showed busloads of women and children departing we scanned them desperately, hoping to catch a glimpse of Alida or her mother, Sulejmana, or Muška, her grandmother. But, although Aza recognised many faces that she knew, those three were not among them.

By now she was in a pit of despair. It seemed almost certain that Alija and Mustafa would be killed, if they had not been already, and she didn't know the whereabouts of the rest of her family, or even if they were alive. Aza had lost the country she loved and all the possessions she had ever owned. In one fell swoop, everyone and everything she loved seemed to have been taken from her.

During that time I watched and listened to every news broadcast. It was all bad and there was nothing to tell me what had happened to my family. Then I heard from Denisa, who had left Zepa with the first bus convoy. She said at that stage my family had still been in Purtići. I didn't want to hear that; if they had stayed on in Zepa they would almost certainly be dead.

Of all the things I'd been through, this period of not knowing was the worst. Luckily I had Brent, who was full of understanding. He did everything he could to comfort me, but he knew Zepa, so he also knew how slim my family's chances were.

Everyone was so kind to me. I would see their faces full of concern – oh, poor Aza! But there was nothing they could do. The air force people sent me flowers; I'll always be grateful for their support, which made me feel that even though I might have lost all my family, at least I still had my friends. And, thank God, I had Brent. Avis and Leanne came up from Christchurch to stay with me during that time; their support meant so much to me.

One day in mid-September my father rang me at work to say that the Red Cross had just delivered a message from Bosnia and he was faxing it through. As the fax emerged I could see that it was from Sulejmana. It said that she and Alida and the grandparents were in Breza, a small town about fifty kilometres from Sarajevo, where they had been 'relocated' by the Serbs. Along with many other refugees they were housed in a building that, before the war, had been a rest home, and they were living off international humanitarian aid. Ominously, I thought, there was no reference to Alija or Mustafa.

I rushed the fax home to Aza, and she identified a sentence I'd missed. 'Call us,' it said, but there was no phone number. I hastily rang Dad and it turned out he'd faxed only one side of the message. On the other was the phone number.

All day I kept ringing that number but I couldn't get through. Finally, that evening, I heard it ringing at the other end. By then I was so confused I almost hung up when a woman answered. I asked for my mother and the woman said, 'Just a moment,' and then my mother was speaking to me. My legs almost gave way; I could hardly believe this was happening. Immediately I asked about my father and brother. 'They are right here, sleeping.'

Had I heard her right? Was I just dreaming all this? 'They're all right? You mean they're there?'

'Yes,' she said. 'It's early in the morning here.'

I rang back when it was evening for them and that time I talked to my brother and father. I talked to everyone. I was crying, but only because I was the happiest person in the world.

Brent was the second happiest. From the look on his face I knew he was thinking, 'At last it really is over and the happy Aza I knew has come back to me.' Poor Brent. It must have been at least three months since I'd even smiled, but now a grin was fixed on my face so firmly it might have been welded there. I was just smiling, smiling, smiling.

Here is my family's story of when the Serbs took Zepa.

The news reports from Srebrenica filled all the people in the enclave with a terror which they knew to be justified. At once my family began to hide food and necessary items in the forest, ready to flee there once again. It was the only place they could hope to hide, but they knew that even the forest wouldn't save them from the Serb weapons of war. The only shred of hope they had was that the outside world would respond to what they were seeing on their TV screens, and UNPROFOR or NATO would step in to save them.

People who had fled from Srebrenica and trekked over the mountains were arriving in Zepa with stories of slaughter and brutality beyond anything that the news reporters had yet presented to the world. (Four of my uncles were among those many men executed and buried in mass graves, or just left where they lay.)

Hearing these stories, my family went far into the forest to hide. Everyone went: my parents, grandparents, little sister, aunt, brother and sister-in-law, and the nephew I'd never seen – Fatima now had a little boy and was expecting her second baby.

When the Serbs came into Zepa, saying that the women and children would be removed on buses, my family had a discussion and decided they must take that chance of surviving. My grandfather, being old, could also go on the bus.

But my father and brother had no doubts about what would happen to them if they stayed in Zepa and surrendered as the Serbs demanded; they would be killed just as my father's brothers and all those other men had been killed.

So they decided that, along with a group of other

men, they would try to escape over the mountain and across Serb territory into the Muslim areas of Bosnia, where it was hoped that those who went on the buses might be relocated. They knew that the odds were heavily against them, but even a ten per cent chance seemed better than certain death.

So, with great sorrow, my family separated, for neither side was expecting to see the others ever again. My grandparents, my mother, my aunt, Alida and Fatima and her little boy walked into Zepa, carrying a blanket each and a few clothes. They had no confidence in the promise of buses to take them away – for all they knew they could be walking to their deaths.

In Zepa thousands of women and children, and old or sick men, stood waiting to be herded on to buses. There were also men of fighting age who were there to give themselves up. My family watched in horror as some of these men were casually executed in front of the terrified crowd. All of us knew those young men. One of them had young children; he'd given himself up in the hope of some day having a future with them. The Serb soldiers were killing these men for no reason, except perhaps that they might breed. Seeing this, my family were certain that my father and brother had made the right choice.

My mother might not have been happy before about my leaving Zepa, but now she was very glad I wasn't there. All those Serb soldiers I had known in my past – perhaps the same ones who had called for me to be given to them in exchange for our villages – would have done to me whatever they wanted.

The people were pushed on to the buses, my family among them. They were leaving their land, their home and almost everything they had ever owned. Now they, too, were refugees – Fatima for the second time in her eighteen years.

At Sarajevo the buses stopped and names of all the people were recorded. They were then allotted the places to which they would be relocated. My family was to go to the town of Breza, which was in a Muslim area in the centre of Bosnia. There they were taken, with other refugee families, to what used to be an old people's home; each family had just one small bedroom in which to live. My mother then sent the Red Cross message to me.

My father and brother set out with a couple of dozen other men to cross the mountain. Theirs was just one of three or four groups intent on escaping, but each group had decided on a different route. Alija and my father had the benefit of knowing the area extremely well. As a boy, Alija had explored the forest and knew it like the back of his hand, while my father, being a bus driver, was very familiar with the roads and countryside beyond the enclave.

Alija was the lead scout for the group on their journey, picking his way though the forest, negotiating mines and enemy locations. After they left the cover of forest, the men travelled only at night, but even so they were sometimes seen by Serb soldiers and had to run and fight for their lives. In doing so, several men in the group were killed.

After three days and two nights, my father, Alija and a handful of their companions reached central Bosnia. Word filtered through that, of the other groups, most of the men had been killed or taken prisoner. My brother and father tracked down the rest of my family and turned up at that rest home in Breza.

My family could hardly believe their eyes – how could they be so lucky? Amid so much horror, my family felt, at that moment, nothing but amazement and joy.

Beneath my smiles there was one continuing sadness.

When I'd talked on the phone to my family, it seemed I'd talked to everyone but my little sister. She took the phone but she was crying so much she couldn't speak. 'Don't cry,' I said. But I was weeping as much as she was.

A little later I rang my family from Christchurch, and tried again to talk to Alida. But mostly she left the talking to me.

'You must be a big girl now?'

'Yes.'

'Are you going to school?'

'Yes.'

Then, when my mother took the phone I could hear Alida, suddenly vocal, saying that she wanted to talk to me. She came back on the phone, her voice hurt and angry.

'Why didn't you tell me you were going? You said you'd never leave without me.'

I tried to explain how impossible that would have been. I said our parents needed her and I couldn't have taken her away from them, but some day when I came to see them all she could come back with me. I didn't know if she believed me. Why should she? I'd told her so often when she was a tiny girl that she and I would always be together.

I felt so bad. The next time I talked to my family and my sister took the phone I was swallowing hard.

'Aza?'

'Yes?'

'Listen,' she said, in Bosnian, 'I'm going to tell you something – in English.'

'Yes?' I waited.

'I love you, small fool.'